# The Kids' Kitchen Takeover

# The Kids' Kitchen Takeover

## by Sara Bonnett Stein

WP WORKMAN PUBLISHING COMPANY

NEW YORK CITY

*Library of Congress Cataloging in Publication Data*

*Stein, Sara.*
  *The kids' kitchen takeover.*

  *SUMMARY: Includes recipes and other projects
and activities that can be done in the kitchen.*
  *1. Cookery — Juvenile   literature.   2. Handicraft —
Juvenile literature.*
  *[1. Cookery. 2. Handicraft] I. Title.*
*TX652.5.S66      641.5'622        75-20382*
*ISBN 0-911104-45-3*
*ISBN 0-911104-46-1 pbk.*


*Workman Publishing Company*
*1 West 39 Street*
*New York, New York 10018*

*"An Open Family Book" created by Media Projects
 Incorporated*


*Illustrations: Sara Bonnett Stein*
*Book Designer: Bernard Springsteel*
*Cover Photograph: Kathryn Abbe*
*Photographs: Dick Frank*
*Typeset: Trade Composition*
*Printed and bound by the George Banta Company*
*Manufactured in the United States of America*

*First printing, November 1975*
        *4   5   6   7   8   9*

To Jamie and Joshua

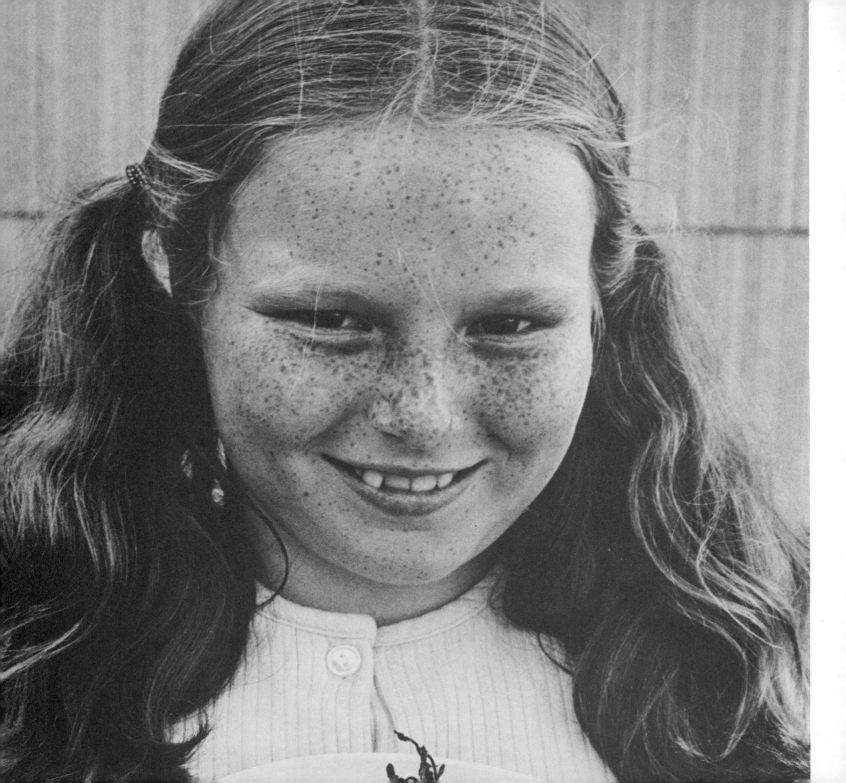

# Contents

# PART 2 — Cooking In The Kids' Kitchen 85

## PART 3 — Life In And Outside The Kids' Kitchen 131

# PART 4 — The Oven Takeover 183

## TO THE PARENTS
# Turning Over The Kids' Kitchen

*The Kids' Kitchen Takeover* is more than a compilation of recipes for children. This book contains a variety of child-tested ideas for hours of pleasure in the kitchen. There are

things to do which require nothing more than supplies found in any pantry; there are experiments with leftovers; there are projects to do outdoors; there are tricks to play; there are pets to keep; there are plants to grow; and, plenty of craft suggestions. Of course there are all different kinds of recipes, some for individual snacks, some for friends and

13

family to share.

The craft, design, and sculpture projects included give the kids freedom to use their own imaginations. We've only mentioned exact amounts, times, and temperatures where it was absolutely necessary. After all, you don't have to knead bread endlessly for it to be good just as you don't have to collect quarts of vegetables before turning them into pickles.

There are enough things to do in this book to interest your children from ages five through twelve. Some ideas can be easily handled by the five year olds, others may involve tools or processes which you feel your child needs some help with. In that case, why not pull up a chair and join in the fun? After all — this is a very democratic takeover.

TO THE KIDS

# Forward Into The Kids' Kitchen

The best time to take over the kitchen is now; and any kind of day can be a good day for kitchen fun.

First check the ingredients and tools you'll need. See what's on hand — for many of the ideas in this book, getting started means gathering up things that are always available. You can turn leftover pits and seeds into small gardens, turn old vegetables that have gone droopy into horrible monsters, perform tricks with eggs or drinking cups, experiment with cornstarch or old half-used birthday candles. There's just no limit to the fun you can have "Just Messing Around" (Part 1) in your kitchen.

Feeling hungry? Part 2, "Cooking In The Kids' Kitchen," has a delicious collection of recipes to try. There are snacks for you to have when you are only feeding yourself, there are treats to make for the whole family or your friends, and there are many recipes which take you back to the old days when people made their own jams, yogurt, or pickles.

When you are lucky enough to spend a day at the beach or in the woods be sure to check through the ideas in Part 3, "Life In And Outside The Kids' Kitchen," before you leave. Days spent outdoors are the days to collect shells, rocks, and sand from the seashore, crickets, plants, and wildflowers from a field or forest. Turn them into kitchen fun when you get home or save them for the next rainy day.

Learn how to make a stove you can really bake in. Or, if you are interested in old stoves, learn how to care for them — you never know, you might be lucky enough to come across one. Then, of course, there's the familiar kitchen stove. Use it to bake potatoes, meringues, cookies, and bread. Part 4, "The Oven Takeover," even explains the ins and outs of starting a small business selling the Portuguese Sweet Bread. But perhaps you'd rather sell the shortbread cookies. Whichever you decide to make all the business information and sales tactics are here.

## Preparing To Take Over

Parents will be willing to let you cook for yourself if you know how to use kitchen equipment and are willing to clean up when you are through. Cooking, even making snacks, is serious business. Hot pots can burn, gas can explode, knives can cut, and parents can get angry with messes. Here are some things to remember.

Having lots of people in the kitchen while you cook is confusing and unsafe, so it's best to make hot foods when there aren't too many friends around. And, it's never safe to cook with really little children under foot.

Read the instructions for each project or recipe thoroughly before getting started. Try to have everything, if possible, within easy reach or at least know where things are so you can work without having to stop to find ingredients. Also by reading through the instructions you will know before you start if there are any steps you don't understand.

Most good, experienced cooks add seasonings to suit their own tastes rather than following exact recipe measurements. We have given exact measurements only when the recipe or project's outcome really depends on it. For instance, a cookie made with too much butter and not enough flour will melt and spread in the heat of the oven and never harden into a cookie. For most recipes, we recommend adding flavorings a little at a time, tasting, and then adding more if it is necessary. After awhile, you will learn how much of something suits you.

Many ideas in this book involve using a knife. Move people out of your way before you use one because cutting anything with other children around you is dangerous. When you cut vegetables or other things direct the knife away from your body, or cut down towards the table surface. This may seem like a clumsy method at first but there are none safer. Be sure to go slowly and watch while you slice.

Obviously, stoves are an important part of cooking. Most people have either a gas or electric model. When you light a gas stove, keep your hand on the burner control knob or oven control knob. Turn the knob for the burner or oven, depending on which you are lighting, to the side. Once the burner or oven is lit, you can adjust the flame to the size you want. If the pilot doesn't light the gas within a

17

couple of seconds, turn the gas off and get an adult to help you. If a match is needed to light the gas, always get help from an adult unless you have permission to light the stove yourself.

Electric stoves have burners that glow bright red only at the highest heats. When it is on low, the burner looks as if it is off. Another point to remember — burners remain hot enough to burn you long after they have been turned off and the red glow has faded. Never, therefore, put your hand on the top of the stove.

When handling cooking pots, always use a potholder. Pots don't look hot, even when they are. Don't make the mistake of using a flimsy shield, like a towel, especially a wet towel, because it will heat through and you'll get burned.

Cooks new to the kitchen tend to use flames which are too high. Their theory seems to be the more heat you use, the faster things will cook. In most cases, the more heat you use, the faster things will burn. Therefore, the recipes included in this book will do just fine on low or medium heat. For instance, a fried cheese sandwich needs low heat to melt the cheese without burning the bread. Cinnamon toast needs a low broiler flame to melt the sugar without burning the toast. Butter will melt on a low heat but will burn on a high

flame. When you stick with low temperatures you can control the cooking of the food better and prevent it from being ruined.

"Doneness" is one of those things learned by experience. If you cook something for ten minutes and it doesn't taste cooked enough when you try it, put it back and cook it a little longer if possible. If it is too well done, cook it less the next time you make it. Generally food is done when it is the texture or color you want it to be, and it seems hot or cold enough.

**The Basics**

If the kitchen is totally new territory, you need to learn some of the basic cooking methods used in this book. If a recipe leaves you in doubt, check these explanations.

*Boiling*. When water is boiling you will see big bubbles rising from the bottom to the top of the pot. You should bring water to a boil over a medium-sized flame rather than a very high flame. This way you lessen the risk of the water boiling over the sides of the pot.

*Simmering*. When the liquid moves as though it will boil any second but no bubbles come up from the bottom of the pot, the liquid is said to be simmering. Once the liquid boils, you can lower the heat to cook it for a long time at the simmering level.

*Hard-boiling eggs*. Eggs have to stay in water that is boiling for ten minutes to become hard. To avoid cracking the eggs, start them in cool tap water and heat gradually to the boiling point, then leave to boil for ten minutes.

*Separating raw eggs*. Tap the egg on the edge of a bowl so it cracks in the middle. Hold the egg with both hands. Place your thumbs close to and on both sides of the crack (if you think you can insert them slightly into the crack without poking the yolk, do it), and gently pull the egg into two pieces over the bowl. Keep the egg tipped slightly to one side so the yolk stays in one half of the eggshell while the white drips down into the bowl. You might have to pass the yolk into the other half of the shell to allow all the white to drip into the bowl. Then the yolk can be put into a separate container.

*Shelling eggs*. Take the pot with the hard-boiled egg still in it to the sink. Run cold water into the pot to cool the egg down. Then tap the egg in several places on a hard surface in order to break the shell. Peel it off with your fingers. Remove the thin membrane found under the shell as well.

**Cleaning Up**

When you are finished working in the kitchen it is important to clean up — all great cooks and artists like to keep their equipment and working space in top condition. So be sure to wipe the mess from the table, counters, sink and stove. Check the floor too for any fallen bits of food.

When washing the dishes and pots and pans remember, hot water gets grease off things much better than cold water. Use enough detergent or soap to make your sponge feel sudsy. You don't have to overdo it, you can always add more.

If, despite a low flame and what seemed like constant attention, a pot was somehow burnt, ammonia poured into it and left for a half hour will loosen much of the crust. The rest of the burnt food takes a steel wool pad and plenty of hard scrubbing.

And now you are ready to take over the kitchen, keeping in mind, of course, that even in a takeover, it's more fun to share. So, when an adult asks for some kitchen time, be gracious. After all, the kitchen can be the best of all family rooms.

# PART 1—
# Just
# Messing
# Around

# Ocean In A Bottle

This toy was for sale as a very fancy, very expensive adult plaything several years ago. It is perfectly simple to make yourself.

You need: **big clear bottle with a good twist top**
**blue vegetable dye**
**mineral or cooking oil (mineral oil looks better because it's clear instead of yellow)**

Fill half the bottle with water. Color the water blue with the vegetable dye. Now fill the bottle to the very top with mineral or cooking oil. Twist the top on tightly. If there are any bubbles get rid of them by taking the top off and over-filling the bottle slightly with either water or oil. Put the top on again. If the bottle is oily, wash it off.

Now place the bottle on its side and you will see a blue "ocean." Rock the bottle to make waves.

# Sink Submarine

**You need:** **scissors**
**3-foot piece of plastic tubing (the kind used in aquariums and available in pet stores)**
**large-mouthed bottle (the kind orange juice comes in)**
**washcloth**

Cut the tubing into one two-foot piece and two six-inch pieces. Don't bother about being exact. Place the bottle on its side. Stick the long piece of tubing into the bottle so that one

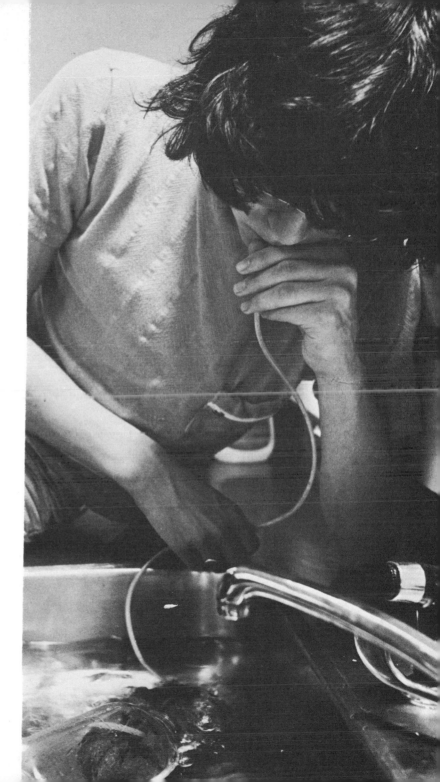

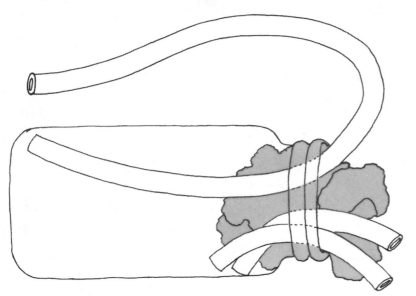

This is the way the tubes should be placed in a sink submarine. Cram the washcloth in very tightly.

end reaches the bottom and the other end hangs out. Push the washcloth into the mouth of the bottle. Now squeeze the two short pieces between the washcloth and the jar and opposite the long piece. They too should stick out, and be next to each other.

Because the tubing comes in a roll, each piece has a curve to it. Holding the bottle on its side, fiddle with the tubes until the long tube curves up and touches the top wall of the bottle. The short tubes should curve down and touch the bottom wall. Be sure the washcloth

is stuffed tightly into the bottle's mouth so the submarine doesn't leak.

Fill the kitchen sink with water and try the submarine out. Place it in the sink and put the long air tube in your mouth. When you blow into it, the submarine will fill with air and rise to the surface, propelled by the bubbles which will come out of the short tubes. When you suck air out of the bottle through the tube, you will pull water into the submarine through the short tubes and it will sink like a real submarine. Blow into the tube again to make it rise.

# Water Equalizer Machine

The water equalizer machine is a way to mess around using the principle of the syphon and the fact that water seeks its own level if it can.

**You need:  2 water glasses**
**1½-foot piece of plastic tubing or more for fancier tricks (purchase this tubing in a pet store that sells aquarium equipment)**

Fill one glass with water. Put one end of the plastic tubing into the water and suck on the other end until water comes through the tube and into your mouth.

Quickly stick a finger over the end of the tubing and take it out of your mouth. Then place the end into the empty glass. The water should siphon from the full glass into the empty glass until the water in both is equal in height.

Now you can fool around with the water equalizer. Add water to one glass and watch the water flow from it into the other until the water in both is equal in height again. Change the levels of the glasses to see if the same thing happens. Try sucking out water from one glass with a basting tube or drink some through a straw.

You can add more glasses and pieces of tubing to your water equalizer machine (the illustration shows how to do this). And experiment with colored water too.

# Antibubbles

A bubble is a drop of air held together by a film of water (or soapy water). An antibubble is just the opposite: a drop of water held together by a film of air.

**You need: liquid detergent**
**2 water glasses**
**eyedropper**

Mix up a solution of detergent and water. It's hard to say how much detergent to use — start with four or five drops for a cup of water. Divide the mixture between the two glasses.

With the eyedropper, draw up some of the solution from one glass and squirt it hard into the other. If the mixture is right, you'll see small antibubbles roll across the surface when you squirt. If you are lucky and keep trying, you may get very large antibubbles. (We've had success using an ear syringe; try it if you happen to have one.) If you get very lucky, one or two antibubbles will be beneath the surface of the mixture and will float around for a minute or so — long enough for you to see the film of air around them clearly.

# Dribbler

Here's a good trick to try on your friends, but practice it in private first because some glasses seem to work better than others.

First challenge them by saying, "I bet I can give ten people a drink of water from their own glasses but only pour water into one glass." This is how you do it.

**You need: 10 glasses or orange juice**
**cans of the same size with**
**straight sides**
**pitcher**

The trick is to arrange the glasses or cans in a pyramid so that as each upper glass overflows, it fills the glasses underneath it. Build the pyramid by placing six glasses in a circle to form the bottom ring, then three for the middle ring, then one for the top. Start pouring water into the top glass. If the glasses are arranged properly the top glass will overflow into the three glasses below it. As they fill up, they will overflow and fill the six glasses under them. Keep pouring. Soon you will have given ten people glasses of water but you will have poured water directly into only one glass.

# Ice Races

Ice skaters can skim across the ice because the pressure of their skate blades melts a thin film of water as they go. The same principle in reverse is true of ice cubes; where they touch a surface, a thin film of water forms, making them very slippery. That's why it's difficult to pick up ice cubes from flat counters.

**You need: ice cubes**
**can or string**

A linoleum, vinyl, or asbestos floor in your kitchen makes a good race track or target practice range for the ice cubes. Set up a can as target or a piece of string as a finish line for ice cube games. The worst that will happen is the kitchen floor will get wet. If so, give it a quick mop when you are finished, and no one will get upset.

# Ice Cups

Here is a reverse way to make a drink cool.

**You need: paper or plastic cup**

Fill the cup with water and put it in the

freezer. Take it out when the water is only partially frozen and the center is still liquid.

Run cool water over the bottom of the cup until the ice slips out. Gently break open the top of the ice cup with a pick or knife, and pour the water out. Now you have an ice cup. Instead of putting ice into water or punch to have a cool drink, you can put water or punch into ice.

# Icebergs

Here is a fun thing to have in the bathtub with you on a hot day.

**You need: plastic bag**
**rubber band**

Fill the plastic bag almost to the top with water. Leave an inch or so of air space above the water level and twist the top tightly, fold it over, and secure it with the rubber band.

Carry the bag, *supporting it from the bottom*, to the freezer. Leave it there overnight. In the morning or when it is frozen solid, take it out, peel the plastic bag off, and you have an iceberg. You can put your iceberg in the bathtub for a cool summer bath, and at the same time observe that, yes, it is true, only a third of an iceberg shows above the water.

# How To Get A Cork Out Of A Bottle Without Touching It

Since this can take several hours, depending on how cold your freezer is and how small the bottle, this is not a dramatic trick. Still, it will do for a slow party, a rainy afternoon, or a long evening.

**You need:  empty soda bottle
cork**

Fill the soda bottle with water. Cork it. Put it in the freezer. As the water freezes, it expands. Out pops the cork — and nobody touched it!

# Zap

As a parent, I have not been able to watch while kids do this trick. I take it from my children that it really works.

**You need:** cup of water
metal pie plate
kitchen match box without
matches
hard-boiled egg
broom

Place a cup of water on a counter. Put a metal pie plate on the cup. Put a kitchen match box standing upright on the pie plate. Balance a hard-boiled egg on the match box.

Now, stand in front of the balancing act and step on the brush part of the broom. Pull the handle back towards you and aim at the pie plate. Let go.

I'm told this is what happens: The broom handle hits the pie plate, the plate and match box fall with a crash, while the egg (believe it or not) slips safely into the cup of water without breaking. Experts do this trick with a raw egg!

# Balloon Blowup

Tell your audience you have a magic bottle that can blow up balloons. Then do this trick.

**You need:** balloon
empty soda bottle
pot with a little water

Put a balloon over the top of a soda bottle. Stand the bottle in a little water in a pot. Put the pot on the stove and heat it slowly. As the air in the soda bottle warms up, it will expand. And as it expands, it will blow up the balloon!

# Spoon Shot

This trick needs some practice to do it perfectly. Exactly how hard you hit the spoon and where you place the glass depend on the shape of the spoons you are using.

**You need: 2 metal teaspoons**
**tin can or glass as tall as the spoon is long**

Put a spoon on the counter and place a tin can or glass near it just as it is in the picture. Then put another spoon handle first under the first one, also as shown. Hit the bowl of the second spoon with your fist. If you do it right, the first spoon will fly up in the air and land neatly in the glass. Do your practicing with a tin can. Try it with a glass when you're pretty sure of yourself.

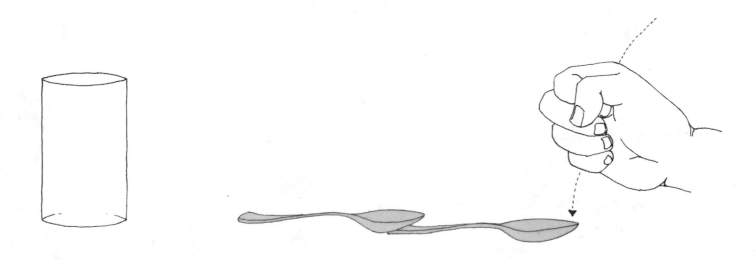

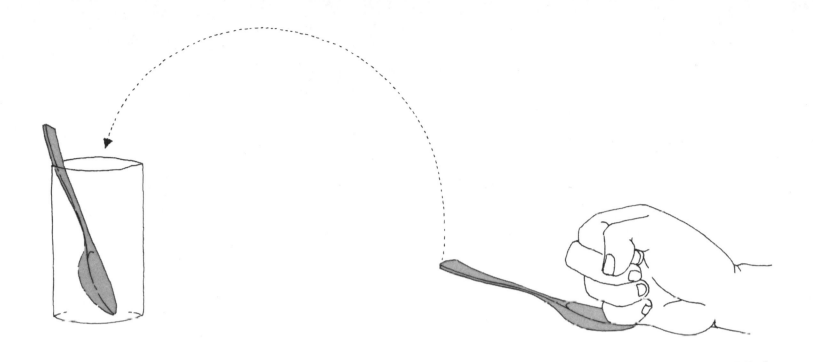

# Burnout

This trick involves a balancing act that most people will think is impossible — two forks locked together and balanced on the edge of a glass by only the tiniest tip of a burned-out match. Set it up ahead of time to make it look even more impressive.

**You need:** **2 metal forks**
**2 wooden matches**
**tall glass**

Lock the tines of two forks together. Insert a match into the top of the tines. Balance the forks on the rim of a tall glass. The balancing point will vary with the type of fork you use. When it's time to do the trick, announce that you can burn the head off the match without disturbing the forks. Light the head of the match with the second match. Let it burn until you think you can knock the head off right at the rim of the glass. Blow out the match and knock off its head. The forks will not fall down, even though only the tiniest tip of the match is now in contact with the rim of the glass.

34

# Burning Sugar

If you take a match or a candle and try to burn a sugar cube, it won't work. Try it.

**You need: matches or candle**
**sugar cube**
**ashes**

Show your audience that sugar alone won't burn. Then take some ashes — from an ashtray, or the fireplace, or burn up some paper to get a supply. Rub the ashes on the bottom of the cube. Now hold a match to it and watch the sugar burn! The reason the sugar burns this time is that the ashes act as a "catalyst" to the sugar. A catalyst is any substance that speeds up a chemical reaction like burning.

# How To Make An Oil Lamp

Before electricity was understood, people often used oil lamps to light their houses. You can make an oil lamp using just ordinary cooking oil. Although the old lamps used

35

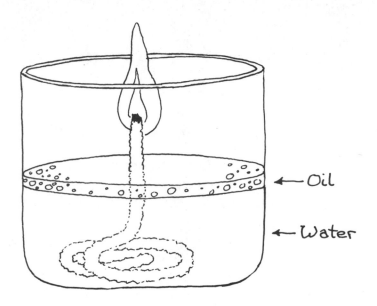

← Oil

← Water

more effective wicks and brighter-burning oils to give off more light, yours will give you an idea of what they were like.

**You need: water glass**
**cooking oil**
**pipe cleaner**

Half fill the glass with water. Pour a thin layer of cooking oil on top of the water. Oil will not dissolve in water and remains floating on it. Curl the end of a pipe cleaner into a coil so it stands up in the glass. Lower the coiled end into the water. The top of the pipe cleaner should be about one half inch above the oil. Don't let this top portion get wet. The pipe cleaner is the wick; light it and you've got an oil lamp.

# Making Candles

There are many different ways to make candles. For the ones we make you start with hot wax.

**You need: paraffin (from a hardware or grocery store) or old candle stubs**
**double boiler or pot with a bowl that fits on top without tipping**

Melt the wax or paraffin in the double boiler or the bowl placed on top of a pot of boiling water. Paraffin and candle wax are flammable so keep the heat low, even if it takes a long time to melt the wax, and be careful about spilling or dripping.

### Hand-Dipped Candles

In the old days, candles were made two different ways. The first was by dipping a long wick into melted wax, letting the wax harden on the wick, then dipping it again, until there were enough layers to make the candle as thick as the maker wanted.

**You need: soft string**
**stick**
**hot paraffin or wax**

You can make candles this way with any soft string tied to a stick. Use the stick as a handle when dipping. The string at the stick end is the wick. Cut the bottom of the candle flat with a knife.

## Molded Candles

The other way people used to make candles was in candle molds. The string hung down into the middle of a mold, and the melted wax was poured in. The molds came apart so the candle could be taken out after it hardened. This is still the way fancy candles are made — the ones that are shaped like pine trees, eggs or pumpkins. If you look, you can usually find the seam where the two halves of the mold were joined.

If you like candles that are interesting shapes, you can make some in a seamless mold in damp sand.

**You need: hot paraffin or wax**
**bucket of damp sand**
**scissors**
**soft string**
**stick that is long enough to rest across the bucket's top**

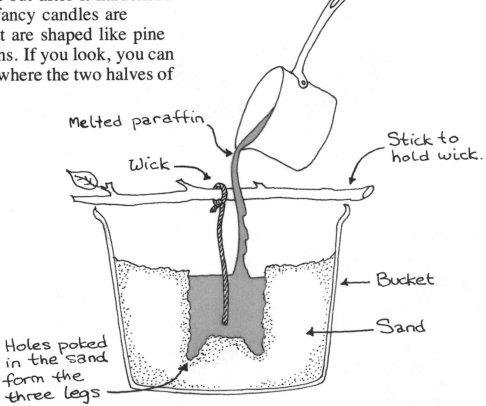

Melted paraffin

Wick

Stick to hold wick.

Bucket

Sand

Holes poked in the sand form the three legs

38

First melt the wax (see the explanation at the beginning of project) over a low flame. Dig a hole in the middle of the damp sand — the sand only has to be a little deeper than the length you want the candle to be. The bottom of the hole will be the bottom of the candle. We made little legs for our candle to stand on by poking a finger into the sand for each leg. The finger holes went deeper than the rest of the candle's bottom so the wax hardened into legs. We made only three legs because with that number you don't have to be too careful about the depth of the holes — the candle will stand up, even if it leans to one side a little.

Cut a length of string long enough to tie around the stick and reach from the top of the bucket to the bottom of the hole in the sand. Tie it to the stick and dip it once in the melted wax so it hangs straight. Rest the stick over the rim of the bucket with the string centered over the hole.

Pour in the melted wax until it fills the hole. If you are making a thick candle, it will take hours to harden. It's hard when you can't see through the middle of the wax. To free the candle, dig around it with your hands, and lift it out gently. Wash the extra sand off and trim the wick to the right length with scissors.

# Wax Pie

Just as the English use leftover meat to make meat pies, you can use leftover wax candles to make wax pies.

**You need:** matches
leftover birthday candles in
different colors
bowl of cold water

Light a candle and drip the melting wax onto the surface of the water in the bowl. The wax will harden into a roundish shape immediately and float. Light another candle and drip it next to the first circle. Keep doing this with different colored candles. Slowly you will make a flat pie of different colors floating on top of the water.

When you think the pie is large enough, lift it out of the water and hold it up to the light to see how pretty the colors are.

# Sandcast Plaster Landscapes

All sorts of gadgets from the kitchen, or tools from the toolbox can be used to make strange sand castings. We like the prongs of a hammer, the bulb end and squirt end of a baster, a flattened corkscrew, the top of a big glue bottle, the handle of a wooden spoon to make holes, and flattened fork tines. Even if the sand castings aren't done very carefully, they look like outer space landscapes.

**You need:** half a bucket of the finest
sand you can find
aluminum baking pan
gadgets, tools, or utensils
plaster of paris or patching
plaster
bowl
large spoon

Pour several inches of sand into the baking pan. Your landscape can only get as high as the sand is deep so if you have a pan or tub deeper than a roasting pan, that would be even better. We used an old galvanized tub.

Dampen the sand until it holds its shape well when you mold it. Then smooth it as flat as you can and tamp it down as firm as you can. Choose the gadgets you like, and press each one carefully into the sand. When you pull it out again, it will leave a clear impression in the sand. When you fill the impressions with plaster, you make the shapes that will stick up from your finished landscapes. Make some of them shallow and others deep, and use objects that have interesting shapes.

Mix the plaster. In case the instructions on the package aren't clear, this is how we do it: Pour cold water into a bowl — start with about two cups, maybe three if you're making

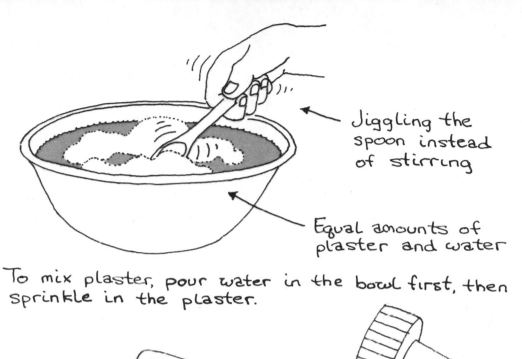

Jiggling the spoon instead of stirring

Equal amounts of plaster and water

To mix plaster, pour water in the bowl first, then sprinkle in the plaster.

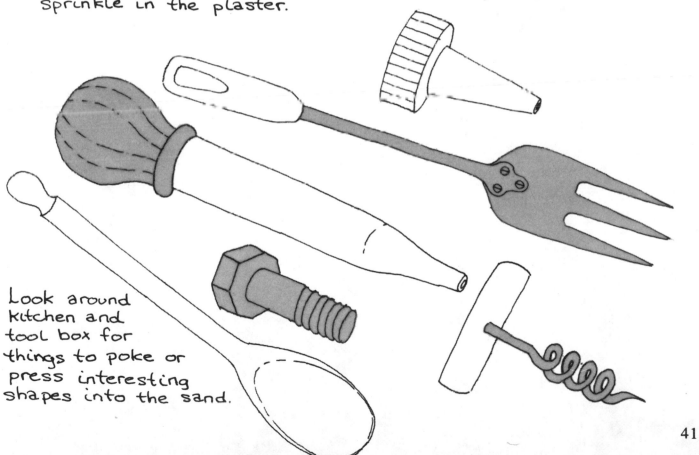

Look around kitchen and tool box for things to poke or press interesting shapes into the sand.

a big landscape. You can always make more plaster if it's not enough. Now pour plaster evenly into the bowl until it is as high as the water. Instead of stirring it, which makes it lumpy, dip a spoon down to the bottom of the bowl and just vibrate it gently for a couple of minutes or even less. Gradually the water will seep evenly into the plaster. The consistency should be about the same as a good milkshake.

With a big spoon, start spooning the plaster onto the sand. Fill up the deep or fragile places first, and don't worry about covering the whole surface until you've finished filling all the holes. When the impressions are covered, just keep spooning plaster over the whole surface. To make your landscape strong the plaster should end up about an inch thick. But you don't have to go to the edges of the pan — leave a margin of sand all the way

around so you don't have trouble getting the landscape out of the pan, or the plaster off its sides. If you've slopped plaster on a good roasting pan, wipe it off now with a sponge before it's hardened.

It will take about an hour for the plaster to get hard enough to lift off the sand. Plaster heats up while it's setting. As long as it feels warm, it won't be hard enough to lift. When it's quite cool, you can test it with a fingernail to see how hard it is. If it scratches easily, wait a little longer.

When the plaster is hard, lift the landscape out of the sand and rinse it. (A little sand won't clog the kitchen drain.) It's surprising to see how much more exciting the landscape looks than the impressions you made in the sand.

All this takes longer to write about than to do. Sandcasting is one of the easiest ways to make interesting things.

# Fake Fossils

Exploring the attic one day, we found a dead rat. Not a new dead rat, but practically a mummy. It might have been there for thirty years. The entire skeleton was still attached — skull, tail, even the little foot bones.

The bones were so delicate that we went out of our way to find really fine sand on the low tide area of the beach (the kind you need to make drip castles); the rest of the casting was as sandcast plaster landscape. We had to be especially careful lifting the bones out of the sand but when it was finished, it looked exactly like a sandstone fossil of some ancient creature.

**You need: dried bones from a chicken or bird, or shells
fine sand
plaster of paris or patching plaster**

Since not just anybody happens upon a dried rat, you could save chicken bones and make up your own prehistoric monster out of them. The only difference is you have to lay the bones in the sand so they look like an animal and then pick them out again one by one. You could make fake fossils from shells too.

# Color Bombs

This project is almost too simple to write about, but it is very beautiful to watch.

**You need: tall clear bottle (an olive jar, for instance)
food coloring**

Take the bottle and fill it with water. Drop in one drop of any of the food colors. Watch it form bombs that hit the bottom, leaving streamers of color that swirl and flow like banners. Add another drop of a different color and another, and another, and another.

# Batik Banners

Batik is a way of dyeing cloth. You make a design on white cloth with melted wax, and then dye the cloth. The dye will cover all but the waxed area, so when the wax is removed from the cloth your design shows in white. Be sure the cloth you use is not too thick. If it is, the wax won't soak into it. Handkerchiefs work, and so do old sheets and pillowcases.

**You need: white rags
waxed paper
breadboard and thumbtacks or stick pins (optional)
paraffin (buy in a hardware or grocery store)
double boiler or pot with a bowl that fits on top**

1. Melt wax in a double boiler. Pin the cloth down over wax paper.

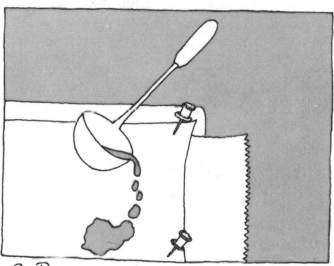

2. Pour your design with a pitcher, spoon or ladle.

**without tipping**
**kitchen spoon, ladle, or small pitcher**
**cold water dye**
**newspapers**
**dull knife**
**iron**
**paper toweling**

Prepare your rag first, so it will be ready to use as soon as the paraffin is hot. Lay the rag you want on a piece of waxed paper so you don't end up scraping wax off the counter or table. If you have an old breadboard or

3. Dye the cloth in cold water dye, and rinse very well.

47

something you can stick thumbtacks or pins into, tack your rag down over the waxed paper; it will be easier to work on.

Now heat the paraffin. If you don't use a double boiler, put water in a pot, put the paraffin in a bowl, then put the bowl on the top of the pot and the pot on the stove. A low heat is safest. You do have to be careful melting paraffin because it can catch on fire. That's why you melt it over hot water instead of directly over a flame. That's also why you should be sure the bowl you are melting it in isn't liable to tip and that no paraffin drips down the sides.

When the paraffin is a thin liquid, it's ready

5. Scrape off the wax with a dull knife.

4. Drip dry over newspaper.

6. Iron the cloth between layers of paper towels.

to use. Move it to where you're working, but keep the bowl on the pot of hot water so the wax stays hot while you work.

The simplest way to make a design is to drip the paraffin from a spoon, ladle, or even a small pitcher right onto the cloth. You can paint the paraffin on with a brush too, but it cools pretty fast on the brush and you may have trouble getting it to soak into the cloth. If the wax looks whitish when it's on the cloth, it's too cool and won't soak in. If it is soaking in right, the cloth will look translucent like a grease spot, and the wax will be on both sides of the rag. If it isn't working try thinner cloth, reheating the wax, or thinning the wax with turpentine.

After you've finished your design, mix the dye according to the directions on the package. Then dye the rag and rinse it, also following the directions on the package. Leave the rag to dry, but not where it will drip on the floor. You can dry it on newspapers, for instance.

When the rag is dry, all you have to do is get the wax off. Scrape off as much as you can with a dull knife. Then iron the rag between four or five layers of paper towel. Ironing melts the wax and the paper towels absorb it.

Now that you're finished, you'll see that almost anything you do by dripping, dribbling, or pouring wax looks good enough for a banner to hang on the wall.

When you are ready to clean up, empty the wax out of the bowl into a storage container while it is still liquid. Scrape as much of the wax as you can off your tools. Then wash everything with detergent and very hot water.

# Pole And Tie Dyeing

There are two other simple ways to dye pretty patterns into cloth.

**You need:** **pole**
**piece of thick cloth**
**rubber bands**
**string**
**dye**
**roasting pan**
**newspaper**

## Pole Dyeing

The first method uses a pole — a thick dowel with a piece of cloth over the end. Pull the cloth tight around the pole like a closed umbrella, and secure it in several places with rubber bands. Now take some string and wind lengths of it around and around the cloth in the places you want to stay undyed. You can wind the string in zig zags too. Mix the dye in a roasting pan according to the instructions on the package. Dye the cloth by putting the whole pole into the dye bath. If the pole is too long and won't fit, hold one end in the pan and pour lots of dye over it. Rinse it according to the package instructions, without removing the cloth from the pole. Hang or prop the pole over newspaper until it has finished dripping. Then untie and spread flat to finish drying.

Little circles can be made by pinching the cloth wherever you like and tying each pinch with rubber bands and then string. If the tips of the pinches were bound, you would get polka dots.

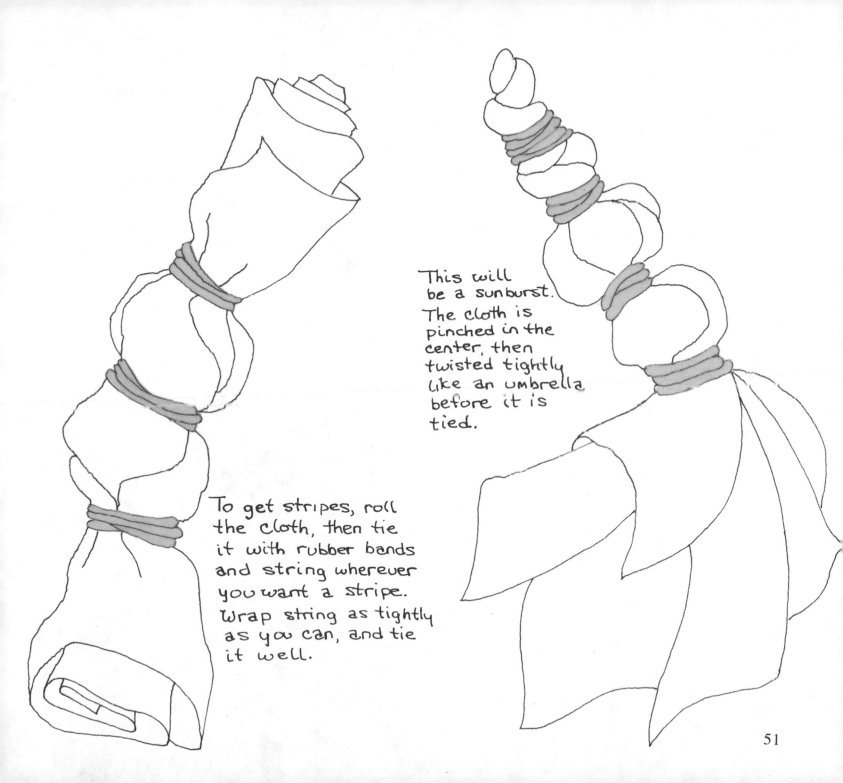

This will
be a sunburst.
The cloth is
pinched in the
center, then
twisted tightly
like an umbrella
before it is
tied.

To get stripes, roll
the cloth, then tie
it with rubber bands
and string wherever
you want a stripe.
Wrap string as tightly
as you can, and tie
it well.

51

### Tie Dyeing

The second simple way to dye cloth is called tie dyeing. There are many special techniques for folding and tying that have been developed to get different patterns, but it might be more fun to develop some for yourself.

**You need:** **string**
**cloth**
**pot or pan**
**dye**

The basic idea is to wind strings around a pleated cloth wherever you want it to stay undyed. You can also tie the cloth in knots at various places. The picture shows how different ways of pleating and tying produce different patterns. Once the cloth is tied, dyeing, rinsing and drying techniques are the same as for pole dyeing.

# Cornstarch Fingerpaint

**You need:** **3 tablespoons cornstarch**
**3 tablespoons cold water**
**cup boiling water**
**liquid detergent**
**vegetable dye or tempera**
**paint**
**shelving paper**

Mix the cornstarch with the cold water first until you have a smooth paste. Stir in the boiling water. Add a squirt of liquid detergent to make the paint easy to clean off things. Color it with vegetable dye or tempera paint. The dye will color your hands a little and could stain clothes too, so be careful. Let the fingerpaint cool before you use it.

Shelving paper, shiny-side-up, makes good fingerpaint paper.

# Cornstarch Goop

The reason this strange mixture behaves the way it does is difficult to explain and understand. It's more fun just to mix it up and enjoy playing with it — so here's how.

**You need: several tablespoons**
                        **cornstarch**
**cup**
**water**

Put a few spoonfuls of cornstarch into a cup. Add water a few drops at a time until the cornstarch is pastey. Now pick up this goop and squeeze it — it's crumbly. Hold it loosely — it oozes through your fingers. It's as though you can change the substance from a liquid to a solid by simply squeezing it.

# Gelatin Glop

Since there is no particular recipe for having fun with gelatin, start with this and experiment on your own.

**You need: unflavored gelatin**
**boiling water**
**plastic container**

Mix some plain gelatin in boiling water as you would to make Jello.® The more gelatin you use in proportion to the water, the more firm and elastic the final glop will be. Try using half the amount of water recommended on a package of gelatin.

Put the mixture in a plastic container in the refrigerator. If you make the glop with plenty of gelatin, you can cut it into little jelly cubes to play with.

The big disk in the photograph was made by pouring the gelatin into a pie plate and lifting it out after it jelled. It lifts out easily with your fingers. You don't have to worry about the mixture not jelling — it will.

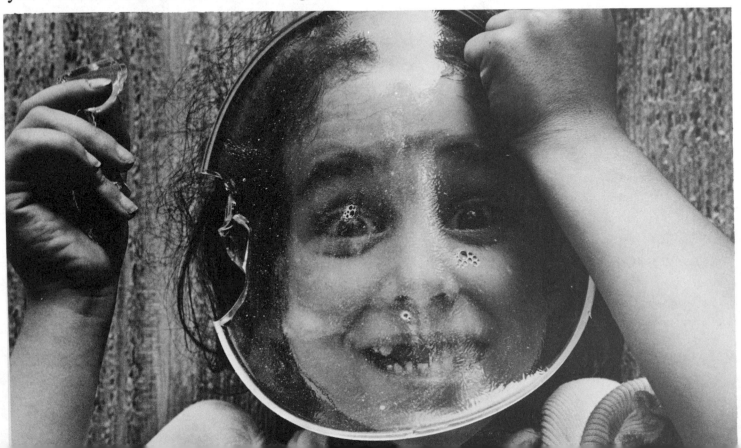

# Vegetable Printers

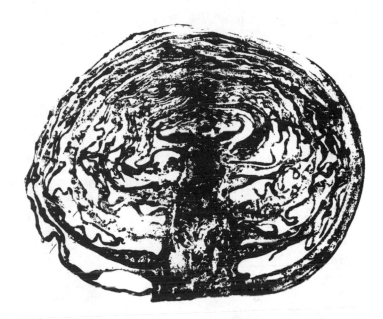

Several different vegetables such as carrots, potatoes, cabbage, or broccoli make fine printers.

**You need: newspaper**
**tempera paints**
**plates or aluminum foil pie**
**pans**
**paper toweling**
**liquid detergent**
**paper to print on**
**raw vegetables**

First cover the surface you will be working on with newspaper. Make sure your tempera paints are nice and thick, and pour a shallow puddle of each color into either a plate or an aluminum foil pie pan lined with several thicknesses of paper toweling. Spread the paint evenly over the toweling to make a stamp pad. Add a few drops of liquid detergent. The detergent enables the paint to stick to slick surfaces such as potato printers. Get out the paper you are going to use. If you feel conscientious about conservation, use old

newspaper. After it's printed, it makes swell gift wrapping.

You can start with a printer as simple as a carrot cut at one end. This will give you polka dots of course. If you cut it on the slant, you get an oval shape. Slice a potato in half. Score out any design you want with the end of a potato peeler or cut out a design by taking chunks out of the potato in spots you don't want to print. A cabbage cut in half makes a huge, gorgeous print. First, though, check if your pan is wide enough for it. A bit of broccoli that is reasonably flat should make an interesting dot pattern. Celery makes little curvy shapes. Try dipping celery leaves into the paint too, and just tap them lightly on the paper. Who knows? Cut a tomato in half crosswise and scoop out the seeds and soft parts. It makes a terrific pattern with the harder parts of the tomato doing the printing. You can clean out the peel of half a squeezed lemon to get a ring pattern from the rind.

To print, just press any of the vegetables onto the stamp pad and then onto the paper.

If you enjoy this type of printing you may want to try the same method with other things. Try cooked spaghetti, string, jar and bottle tops, pieces of sponge, plastic meat trays from the market, crumpled aluminum foil, string or sponge dish mops, the dull side of cookie cutters and plastic forks.

# Fish Prints

The most beautiful prints are made from whole fish before they have been scaled, gutted, definned, or decapitated.

**You need:** **whole fish that no one intends to eat**
**linoleum block ink and roller (from an art store)**
**aluminum pie pan**
**paper**

To pick up all the fine detail of a fish's texture, it is best to use linoleum block ink. Dry the fish very carefully before you roll the ink on it. Pour a small amount of ink into the pie plate. Roll the roller in the ink and then on the fish. Press the fish onto the paper as you would the vegetable printers.

Remember, you can't eat linoleum block ink, so be sure you use a fish that no one intends to eat.

# Roller Printing

There is a way to do roller printing using cardboard tubes from paper toweling and toilet paper rolls.

**You need:**  paper toweling or toilet paper
                              tube
                       grease clay or plasticene
                              (from a dime or toy store)
                       paint brush or piece of
                              sponge (optional)
                       tempera paints
                       liquid detergent
                       plate or aluminum foil pie
                              pans
                       paper toweling
                       newspaper or plain paper
                       string
                       liquid white glue

Next time you finish a roll of paper toweling or toilet paper, save the cardboard tube. Cover it with grease clay. Make a grease clay design on the tube. Prepare the tempera paints by adding a few drops of liquid detergent to each color after pouring them into pie tins lined with paper toweling. Brush paint over the paper tube with a paint brush or smear it on with your fingers or piece of sponge. Roll the tube onto the paper. You can do the same thing with a string wrapped in a pattern over the tube and stuck on with white glue.

# Clove Oranges

Oranges stuck full of cloves smell wonderful. Use navel oranges, not juice oranges.

**You need:**  tin of whole cloves
                       navel orange
                       thimble
                       ribbon (optional)

Press as many cloves into the orange as you can. Your fingers will hurt after the first few cloves so wear a thimble when pushing them in. Be sure you get the cloves close together. They keep the orange from rotting as well as adding spice to the scent.

A ribbon criss-crossed around the orange and tied in a bow at the top turns a clove orange into a good holiday present. It will dry slowly, but still scent a drawer or a closet for at least a year.

# Orange Peel Teeth

Probably nothing draws more groans and gives grownups a bigger surprise than a kid smiling to reveal some gruesome form of play teeth. These are easy to make and you get to eat a juicy orange in the bargain.

**You need:  paring knife**
             **orange**

Cut an orange into sections that are small enough to fit over your teeth but large enough to stay inside your lips when you smile. Eat the orange and tear away any pulp that's left on the rind with your fingers. The inside of the skin will be white. Carefully slit the skin lengthwise down the center of the piece. Leave the peel attached at both ends. Now make short cross cuts on both sides of the slit to form the teeth. Put it in your mouth inside out so the white part shows. Now go out and grin at everybody.

# Presliced Bananas

This is a painstaking trick to prepare for but the effect is terrific: You hand someone a whole unpeeled banana, make slicing motions with your hand while saying appropriate magical words; announce the banana is now sliced inside the unbroken skin and, sure enough, when the banana is peeled, the fruit has been magically sliced.

**You need:  thread**
             **long needle**

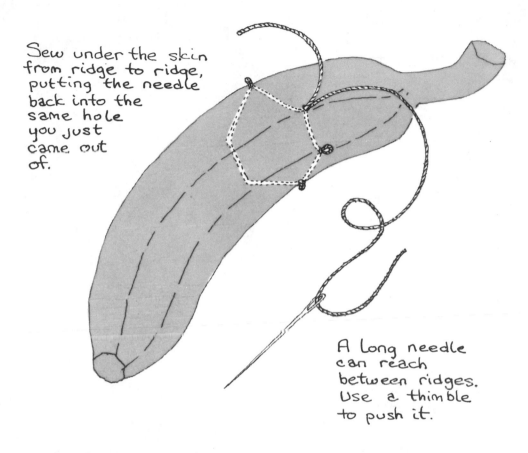

Sew under the skin from ridge to ridge, putting the needle back into the same hole you just came out of.

A long needle can reach between ridges. Use a thimble to push it.

### ripe banana with its skin on

Stick the threaded needle into a ridge of the banana skin at the first point you want to make a slice. Run the needle under the skin from that ridge to the next one, leaving a couple of inches of thread sticking out where you started. Now put your needle back through the same hole it just came out of, slide it under the skin and out the *next* ridge. Keep making invisible stitches until you come back to the beginning and the hole you started at. You now have a neat loop of thread that's under the skin of the banana, but around the fruit itself. If you pull on both ends of your thread the loop will cut right through the fruit and come out the tiny needle hole to make the first slice — and the holes in the ridges should be almost impossible to see.

You may find the slicing very tedious so perhaps it would be best to make your first slice in the middle of the banana and tell your audience the magic will cut the banana in half without touching the peel.

Remember how many slices you make because the trick is even more astounding to your audience if, as you make cutting motions with the side of your hand over the unpeeled banana, you say, "One slice, two, three, four, five . . . this banana is now magically sliced into six separate pieces." And, it is!

# Crow Quill Pen

Long before there were ballpoint or fountain pens, people wrote with pens made from feathers. You can probably use almost any feather you find, but we happened on some crow feathers. Since there is still a kind of artist's pen called a crow quill, we figured crow feathers must be particularly good. They were. At least they don't crack as easily as chicken feathers.

**You need:** **sharp knife**
**feather**
**pin**
**nail file**
**fountain pen ink**

Use a sharp blade to cut the tip slantwise.

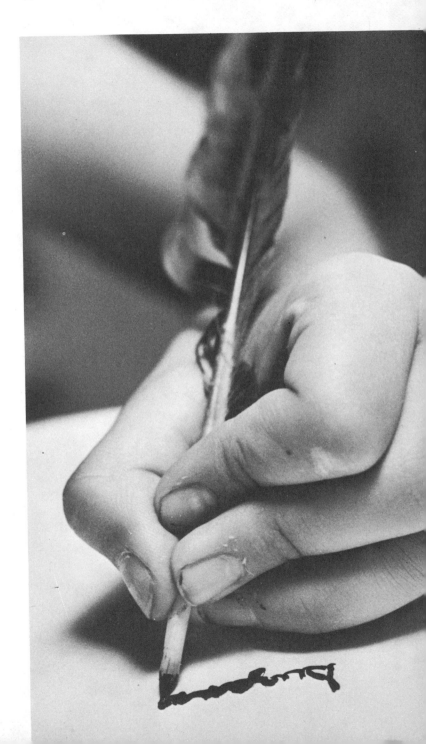

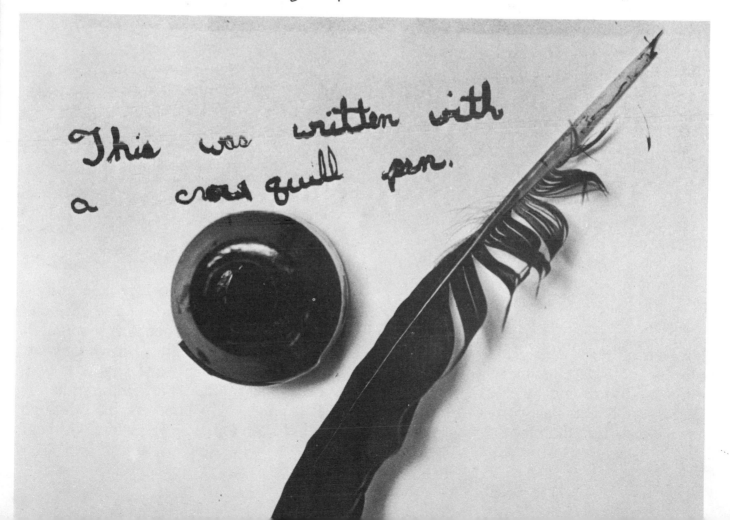

This is the way
the bottom is cut
off the feather to
make a quill pen.

This was written with
a crow quill pen.

The inside of the feather shaft is hollow but it has some thin partitions. Scrape them out (it's easy to do) with a pin. The cleaned, hollow area holds the ink. The best way to get a sharp point on the pen is to file it with a nail file. You can do it with a knife too but it's hard to cut evenly. Slit the point, slightly, up the center.

Use ordinary ink. When you try writing with your pen you'll understand why people needed blotters in the days of quill pens.

# Invisible Ink

Lemon juice, milk, white vinegar and probably quite a few other fluids work well as invisible inks.

**You need:** **quill pen, toothpick, or paper clip**
**lemon juice, milk, or white vinegar**
**iron, lamp, or toaster**

Dip a quill pen, artist's pen (the kind with a wooden handle and changeable pen points), toothpick, or paper clip into any of the liquids mentioned. Write your message. When your friend wants to read what you have written, he or she should iron the piece of paper with a warm iron, hold it over a lightbulb, or a hot toaster until the writing shows. Serious message disguisers usually write innocent notes first with a regular pen leaving space between the lines for the hidden message.

# How To Blow An Egg

According to my grandmother, you don't blow an egg, you suck it. That means you eat the egg raw, something people apparently used to love to do. All that's left of the practice so it seems is the expression ''That's like teaching your grandmother to suck eggs.'' We blow them.

**You need:** **large needle**
**raw egg**
**small dish**

With a needle, poke a tiny hole in the narrow end of an egg. Poke a larger hole in the bottom. This is easier than it sounds if your egg isn't too fragile. Brown eggs are usually stronger than white eggs.

Put a dish on the table. Holding the egg over the dish, blow good and hard through the small hole on top. The egg white will begin to

ooze out of the larger hole in the bottom, followed by the yolk.

Now you can paint or decorate the egg shell or have an egg throwing contest. Whoever breaks the shell is the loser. Obviously the best time to do this project is when you'll be using the egg itself for cooking.

# Silver Egg

Did you ever think you could turn an ordinary hard-boiled egg into a silver egg? It's really simple.

**You need:** **matches**
**candle with a long smudgy wick**
**wire loop from an egg-dyeing packet or kitchen tongs**
**hard-boiled egg**
**water glass**

Light the candle and with the wire loop or kitchen tongs hold the hard-boiled egg high over the flame where smoke forms. Turn it until the egg is covered quite evenly with soot. It will look black and ugly.

Fill a glass with water. Gently drop the egg in and watch it appear to turn bright silver. If you look closely, you can see that the silver is really a thin film of air trapped by the soot.

# Crush

Just for fun, find somebody who thinks he or she is really strong. Say, "I bet you can't even crush a raw egg with one hand." They'll probably answer, "Aw, that's a cinch."

**You need: raw egg**

The fact is, if you hold an egg in the palm of your hand with your fingers wrapped around it, even if you try to crush it with all your strength, the egg won't break. This is because the shape of your cupped hand is similar to the oval shape of the egg. All the pressure you put on the egg is spread so evenly that there isn't enough at any one point to break the shell.

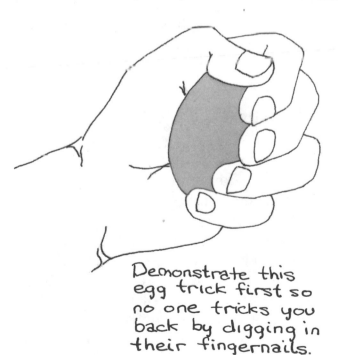

Demonstrate this egg trick first so no one tricks you back by digging in their fingernails.

# Spin

If anyone in your home ever gets hard-boiled eggs mixed up with raw eggs, here's how to sort them out. Take the mixed-up eggs. Spin them, one at a time. The raw eggs will hardly spin at all. The hard-boiled eggs will spin easily. This is because the yolk and white in a raw egg don't spin as fast as the shell and so slow the egg down. Use this principle to perform a trick.

**You need: raw and hard-boiled eggs**

Ask your audience to mix up a few raw eggs with a few hard-boiled ones. Ask if they can now sort the raw from the cooked. When they can't — you can!

# Floating Egg

Eggs don't float in tap water. If you drop an egg into a glass of water it will sink to the

bottom. But if you pour salt into the water, sooner or later the egg will rise to the surface and float. This is because salt water is denser than fresh water. You may have noticed that you, as well as eggs, float more easily in the ocean than in a pond.

**You need: glass with hot water**
               **egg, raw or cooked**
               **salt**

Fill a glass with hot water. More salt will dissolve if the water is hot and the trick will work faster. Lower an egg into it and watch it sink to the bottom. Now, add salt to the hot water. The water will get cloudy from the salt, but the egg will now float.

# Onion Dyed Eggs

Vegetable dyes, like the ones you can buy to dye eggs with, really do come from plants. But you can go right to the plants themselves to dye eggs. Onion skins make beautiful eggs — not evenly colored but mottled like marble, and each egg comes out different. Many stores have bins of onions which are the best places to find lots of skins. They accumulate in the bottom of the bin and the store usually will let you take them without buying any onions.

**You need:** cheesecloth, cut in six- or seven-inch squares
outside papery skins of yellow, Bermuda or red onions
hard-boiled white eggs
small rubber bands
pot of boiling water

**clear varnish spray (optional)**

Lay out a square of cheesecloth. Put some onion skins on it, and nestle the egg in the middle of the skins. Pull the corners of the cheesecloth up over the egg, and fuss with the skins a bit so they go all the way around the egg.

Fasten the cloth together in a bunch at the top with a rubber band. It won't matter if some of the egg isn't covered, because it will show up white and be pretty anyway. When you've gotten as many eggs as you want ready to dye, drop them one by one into boiling water, and boil them for ten minutes.

Then run cold water into the pot to cool the eggs so you can handle them. Take off the cloth and there you are.

The eggs will be mostly an amber-tan color, but some will have green streaks in them, or red or bits of clear yellow. We've never been able to see any difference in the results between using red or yellow onions though, and can't predict whether we'll get any green streaks. The eggs are so beautiful you may want to give them to people as decorations. They'll last for a very long time if you spray them with clear varnish, and if no one breaks them.

# How To Hatch An Egg

Most hens don't hatch their own eggs anymore. They are hatched by the thousands in incubators.

**You need:** **shoebox**
**40-watt bulb**
**socket and cord**
**thermometer**
**aluminum foil**
**cup of water**
**fertile egg**

A homemade incubator can be constructed from a small box (shoebox size) heated by a 40-watt bulb attached to a socket and cord and inserted through a hole at one end of the box. Cut the hole slightly smaller than the socket, and position it about halfway down one end of the box. Insert the socket from the outside of the box, and then screw the bulb on inside the box. Check to make sure the bulb is not touching the box. You will need a

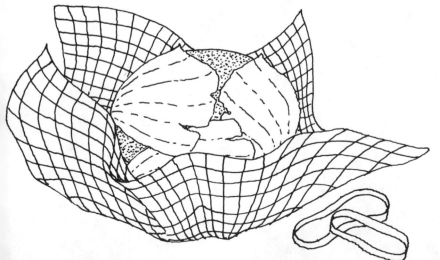

thermometer to check the temperature — it should be kept at 100°. If you can't get the temperature to stay this high, line the box with aluminum foil to act as a heat reflector. You will need some ventilation too. Punch holes in the top. Include a cup of water to add moisture to the air inside your incubator.

Now for the egg. Fertilized eggs can often be bought at health food stores. Or if you live in the country, any farm with chickens should be able to provide a fertilized egg. Naturally, you should start incubating the egg the same day the hen has laid it. The egg has to be turned once every day. The incubation period is about twenty-one days. The hatching process is fantastic to watch. The chick will first peck a small hole in the egg, and then work at it until the egg cracks open. When it first comes out, it will be wet, limp, and look almost dead. That's normal — for a chick.

A newly hatched chick will start to peck for food as soon as it has the strength to stand. Chick mash is available at feed stores and some hardware and pet stores. The chick will need water too.

But what do you do with a full grown chicken? You can't let it live in the house. You can't give it to a neighboring farm, or even a zoo, because it will not know the ways of chickens, and will get clobbered by the

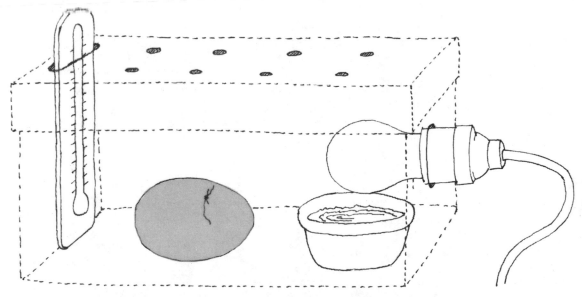

Be sure the bulb is not too close to the cardboard. If the cardboard scorches it could also catch fire.

other hens and roosters. The only thing you can do with a pet chicken is keep it in the yard, either free (if no one minds it scratching holes to take dust baths) or in a small pen. The chick needs a roof over its head at night. If you were lucky enough to hatch a hen instead of a rooster, she will lay more eggs for you, and you'll have food for breakfast.

# Rubber Egg

This is definitely one of the strangest objects to touch.

**You need: raw egg**
                   **drinking glass**

**vinegar**
**bowl**

Put the egg into a glass full of vinegar. Leave it there for one to two days. The vinegar, which is an acid, will dissolve the shell leaving the raw egg inside a thin rubbery membrane that is just underneath the shell. There is no way to describe how weird this thing feels (especially to someone who has their eyes shut and doesn't know what it is).

If there are still fragments of shell left after a couple of days in the vinegar, they can usually be scraped off with a fingernail if you're careful not to break the membrane. The egg should then be kept in a bowl in case it breaks.

After a few days the white from inside the egg will partially evaporate through the pores of the membrane making the whole thing feel soggy. At this point, it's time to throw the egg out. By the way, your rubber egg will feel cold and clammy because the membrane surrounding it is porous and a small amount of the liquid white is evaporating from it all the time.

# Bendable Bone

A bendable bone is made the same way as a rubber egg — by soaking it in vinegar. The acid in vinegar dissolves most of the calcium from the bone leaving only the elastic connective tissue. The bone becomes soft and bends.

**You need:  chicken bone**
**vinegar**
**glass**

Next time you have chicken for dinner save some of the bones instead of throwing them out. For a drumstick, the process takes about two weeks. It takes less time for a wishbone. Put enough vinegar in a glass to cover the bone you choose. Test it every so often to see how it's doing. Don't substitute the rubber wishbone for a real one with little kids because they believe in wishes and will be very disappointed.

# Bone Macrame

The following necklace is made from seagull bones, but you could do the same thing with chicken bones. Wing bones are a good size. Vertebrae from chicken necks are especially good to use as beads because they have holes through them for the spinal cord.

**You need:  chicken wing and neck bones**
**clear varnish spray**

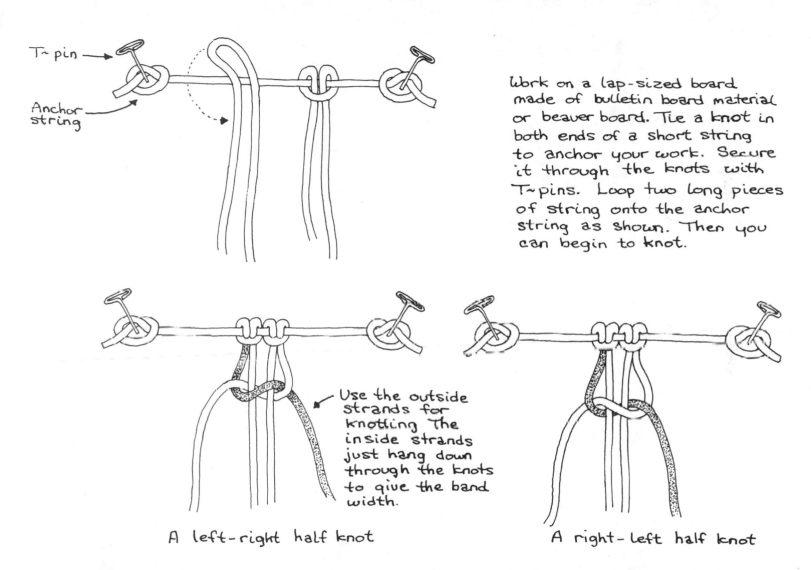

T-pin

Anchor string

Work on a lap-sized board made of bulletin board material or beaver board. Tie a knot in both ends of a short string to anchor your work. Secure it through the knots with T-pins. Loop two long pieces of string onto the anchor string as shown. Then you can begin to knot.

Use the outside strands for knotting. The inside strands just hang down through the knots to give the band width.

A left-right half knot

A right-left half knot

When either of these half knots are repeated over and over, the result is a twisted or spiral band. When the two half knots are alternated (left-right, then right-left) the result is a flat band.

**tackboard**
**T-pins**
**cord for knotting**

To clean the bones, boil them until all the meat comes off easily. Let them dry for a week or so. If you want them to look polished, spray them with several coats of varnish. Then you can make up your own ways to use them in macrame. A book on macrame will tell you more, but the illustration shows the basic knots.

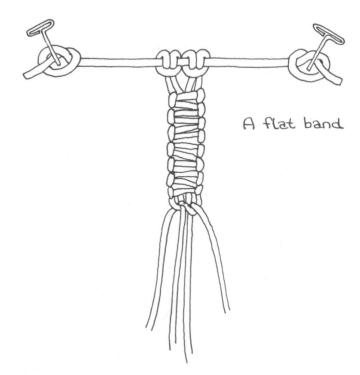

A flat band

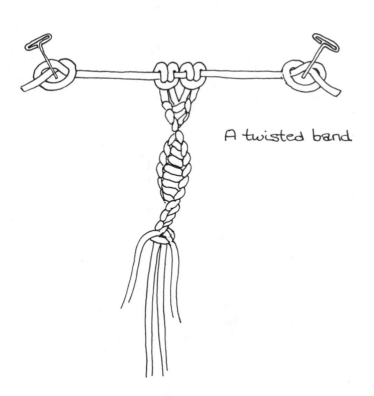

A twisted band

# Noodling

The Italians, who invented most of the shapes for noodles, call any kind of noodle or macaroni or spaghetti pasta. But each sort of pasta has a name of its own. Most describe their shape — spaghetti (string), rigatone (grooved), linguine (tongue), manicotti (small muff), conchiglie (shell), fusilli (twist), penne (pen). Because of their different shapes, pasta make pretty decorations and jewelry.

## Making A Wreath

**You need: cardboard or carton**
**pencil and compass or 2**
   **different-sized plates**
   **(optional)**
**scissors or knife**
**liquid white glue**
**pasta**
**gold or silver spray paint**
**something to punch a hole**
   **with**
**string**

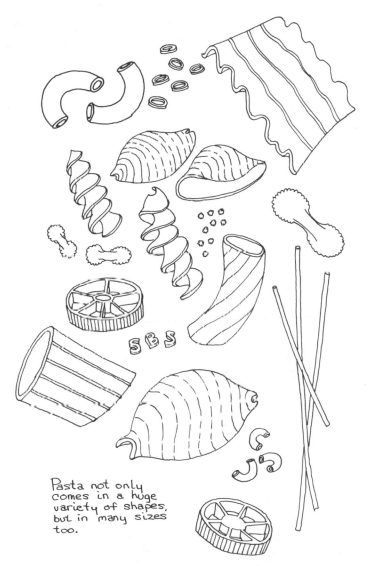

Pasta not only comes in a huge variety of shapes, but in many sizes too.

Shirt cardboard is big enough for a small wreath. If you want to make a large wreath, use the side of a corrugated carton. Draw two circles on the cardboard to form the base of the wreath using a compass, two different-sized plates or free hand. Either the compass or the plates will give you perfect circles, but you can probably do almost as well by hand. Cut the circles out with a scissors, or a knife if the cardboard is really thick. If they are lopsided just let pieces of pasta stick out over the edge here and there to make the wreath look more even.

Make a puddle or drop of glue wherever you want to put a piece of pasta. Then stick on the pasta. First cover all the cardboard, then add more pieces of pasta wherever they will add to the texture or design. The wreath looks more natural if the edges are a little rough and uneven. Leave one small place somewhere near the edge uncovered so you can punch a hole through the cardboard later.

When the glue is dry, spread newspaper over a big area of the floor and spray the wreath with silver or gold paint, following instructions on the can.

Punch a hole through the piece of cardboard you left bare and tie a string through it to hang your wreath.

**Small Ornaments.**

Ornaments for a Christmas tree should be small. If they are too heavy they will pull the

The star is decorated with pastina on both sides. Wheels can be glued to both sides of a round piece of cardboard. The elbows are glued to a round shape too.

branch down. Larger ornaments can be hung in windows. You can make them using the same materials and procedure you used in making the wreath.

If shirt cardboard is too hard to cut into different shapes, use heavy paper. The glue and pasta will make it stiff and strong. Don't forget to leave a bare place for a hole.

**Candle Holder**

**You need:** scissors
cardboard
thumbtack
candle
pasta
liquid white glue
small dish
spray paint

Cut a circle out of a piece of cardboard. Then push a thumbtack through the center and press the candle onto the point. If you don't have a thumbtack or if the candle is too tall for a tack to support, try to hold the candle steady with one hand while you pile pasta around it with the other. It may be easier to do this balancing act if you dip each piece of pasta in a small dish of glue, rather than squeeze glue onto the cardboard each time.

You may have to hold the candle quite a while until the pasta is piled high enough and the glue is set. Then you should be able to lift the candle out gently so you can spray the holder with paint.

## Pasta Jewelry

**You need: newspaper**
**waxed paper**
**pasta with holes through it**
**thin wire (the kind on a spool**
**works best)**

Cover the surface you will be working on with a few sheets of newspaper. Put down a layer of waxed paper on top of them to keep the pasta from sticking to the newspaper when they are sprayed. Spray the pasta on all sides with paint now because it will be too hard to cover them after you've made a bracelet or necklace. When the paint is dry, poke a piece of wire through as many pieces of pasta as you want. Cut the wire to the right length for a bracelet or a necklace. Make the jewelry big enough to fit over your hand or head because trying to make a catch that opens and closes is a nuisance, and it doesn't usually work. Twist the ends of the wire together to hold it shut.

## Noodle Sculptures

Free-form sculptures look pretty the way they are so don't bother to spray them.

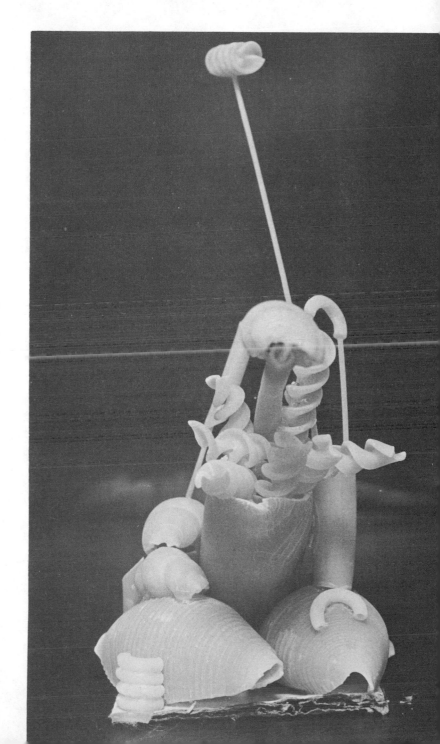

**You need:** scissors
cardboard or wood
various kinds of pasta
liquid white glue

Cut a base from cardboard or use a piece of wood. Decide what kinds of pasta might look interesting together, and begin by glueing down a few pieces that can support others. Large tubular pastas are easy to use. Long thin ones can be propped against one another like a tepee, and held in place until the glue sets well enough for them to stand alone.

Once there is a strong base, embellishing your sculpture with smaller pieces will be quite easy, though you may still have to hold something in place for a minute or so. Often the less glue you use, the quicker the pasta will stick. Some people put a dot of glue on both the sculpture and the next piece to be used, let the spots get tacky, and then join them.

# Bean Pictures

**You need:** cardboard or wood scraps
pencil or pen
liquid white glue
several kinds of beans such
as brown or orange

**lentils; kidney, navy, or
black beans; green or
yellow split peas
any pits or seeds such as
peach or plum pits;
popped or unpopped
popcorn; rice; parakeet,
sunflower, caraway,
mustard, or poppy seeds**

Use the cardboard or wood scraps as a base for your bean picture. Draw your design on it in pencil or pen. Now decide where you want to put each kind of bean or seed. The trick to making bean pictures is to put the glue exactly where you want it for only one kind of bean or seed at a time. For instance, if you want a circle of black beans around bright yellow popcorn, squeeze glue from the bottle around the outside of the circle. Place the black beans on the glue outline. Wait until it dries. Then cover the middle of the circle with glue (you'll have to spread it with your fingers a little) and pour the popcorn on it. When the glue has dried, shake off the extra popcorn. Now go on to the next piece of your picture. Your picture is finished when it looks right to you.

# Vegetable Monsters

Vegetable monsters don't last very long but they are fun and you can always eat the vegetables after you're finished playing.

**You need: toothpicks**
**carrots, beets, potatoes,**
**string beans, peppers,**
**radishes, celery, cabbage,**
**or other vegetables**
**oranges, lemons, raisins, or**
**other fruits**
**cloves**

Use toothpicks to stick one vegetable part onto another. Sometimes you may have to break a toothpick in half to get it a good length but the blunt end will go into a vegetable like a potato and then you can use the sharp end for a vegetable like a carrot. Use the raisins and cloves for eyes and other details.

# Vegetable Flowers

There are a few easy tricks that turn raw vegetables into flowery decorations. They all need a sharp knife, so be very careful.

**You need: sharp small knife**
**carrots, radishes, scallions,**
**tomatoes, turnips, beets**

*Carrot flowers.* With a sharp knife, cut grooves down the length of a carrot. Now when you slice it, each slice will have petals.

*Radish buds.* Carefully slice the red skin of a radish down from the tip towards the stem end, stopping just short of the stem. Repeat until you have red petals all the way around the white bud of the radish.

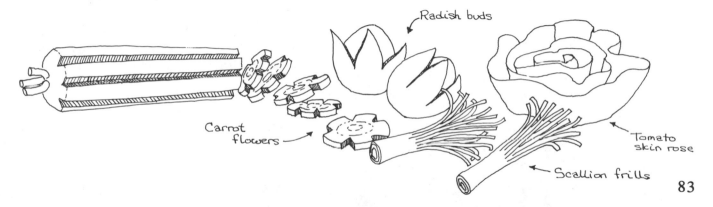

Carrot flowers

Radish buds

Tomato skin rose

Scallion frills

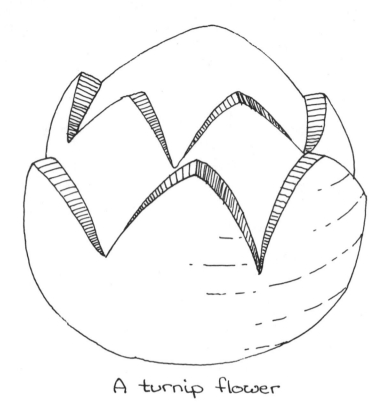

A turnip flower

*Scallion frills*. Choose scallions that don't have a big bulb at the bottom. Cut the root and the green stem off leaving just a couple of inches of white stalk. Slice about an inch into one end as many times as you can so that the end looks like a slightly curly brush.

*Tomato skin roses*. Peel the skin off a firm tomato in a continuous strip going around the tomato the way some people peel apples. When the strip is finished, coil it around and around in the palm of one hand. Spread the "petals" out a little to make it look like a rose.

*Turnip and beet flowers*. This is quite hard to do and your first attempts probably won't look too good. The knife you use has to be sharp and pointed. Peel the beet or the turnip. Cut the stem end flat so your flower will sit straight when it is finished.

With the point of your knife, cut a petal-shaped line all the way around near the bottom of the vegetable. Make the line deeper after you're sure you like the way it looks. A quarter of an inch is right for a fairly large turnip or beet.

Now whittle the vegetable down from the top until the first row of petals stands out clearly. The safest way to do this is to use a cutting board. Stand up and cut the vegetable on the side away from you. Keep your fingers out of the path of the knife and cut small slivers, not big chunks. Repeat this again on a second row of petals. Shape the top like a bud. Whittle here and there until you are satisfied with the shape of the flower.

# PART 2 —
# Cooking
# In The
# Kids'
# Kitchen

# Takeover Apron

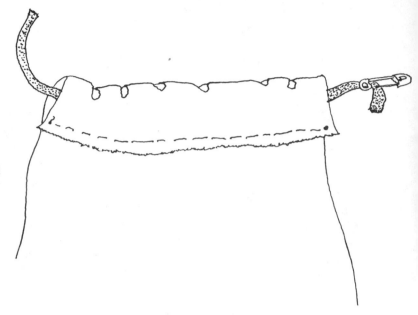

Other than a man's old shirt with the sleeves cut down, this apron is the easiest to make. It can be worn around the waist, or tied around the neck with a second string used to hold it in at the waist. Without decorating, it takes half an hour to make — even for someone who has never sewn anything.

**You need: one yard white cotton fabric,**
**36 inches wide**
**needle and thread**
**scissors**
**3 yards of string, ribbon,**
**seam binding or twill tape**
**big safety pin**
**acrylic paints and brush if you**
**want to paint the apron, or**
**you can decorate it by**
**tie dyeing (page 52) or**
**batik**

The piece of cloth is already the right size. You don't have to do any more cutting. If you don't think you will want to decorate your apron, buy fabric with a pretty color or print. Use the selvage edges of the cloth as the sides. They don't ravel, so you don't have to hem them. Don't hem the bottom either; let it ravel to make fringe.

Fold down the top about three inches from the edge. If there is a "good" side of the cloth, it should be the front. Sew the fold down near the frayed edge using any kind of stitch you know. There will be an opening left through the fold for the tape. Finish the sewing with a couple of tiny stitches so your thread won't pull out. Cut the extra thread off.

The easy way to run the tape or string through the fold is to tie or pin it to a big safety pin. Then push the safety pin through the opening. The string will follow. When the string is through, remove the pin. Tie the apron around your neck, and let it bunch down your front like a halter top. Tie another string to hold it around your waist.

If you want to paint pictures on the apron, use acrylic paints thinned until they are the consistency of a milkshake. Acrylic paints won't wash off in the laundry. You can also dye the apron by the tie dyeing or batik methods.

# Dill Pickles

The easiest way to make dill pickles is to pickle cucumbers right in sterilized quart jars. But there is no excitement in that. This is the way to make dill pickles in a crock. If you don't have one, use a bowl, an enameled pail, or a very big jar.

Pickling cucumbers are small (about four inches long) and should have been picked no more than twenty-four hours before you want to use them. You can get them in grocery stores and at roadside stands during late summer and early fall.

Obviously you can't make dill pickles without dill which is not always easy to find. Dried dill will look messy on your pickles, and dried dill seed will not give much flavor. The flower ends of the dill plant are best for pickles, but stores tend to sell it too young — before it has flowered. It's okay to use anyway.

Dill pickles are pickled (preserved) in brine (salty water) and ferment (become tangy and slightly acid) through the action of yeasts.

**You need:** **cucumbers (buy enough to fill your container two-thirds full)**
**crock or bowl**
**seasonings including dill, several peeled and sliced garlic cloves, whole black peppercorns, some bay leaves**
**brine (2 cups salt and 2 cups vinegar to every 2 gallons of hot water)**
**large pot**
**plate to cover pickles**
**rock or weight to hold down plate**
**quart jars**

First make the brine. You will need about half as much brine as you have cucumbers. For example, if you have half a crock of cucumbers, you will need a quarter crock of brine to cover them. Boil the brine mixture in a pot to dissolve the salt.

Rinse the cucumbers in cold water. Put a layer of cucumbers in the crock or bowl, then sprinkle some dill, garlic and pepper over them. Now add another layer of cucumbers, and then more of the same seasonings (add in a bay leaf or two if you'd like). Keep adding layers until you use up your ingredients. Don't fill the container too full because as the pickles ferment, the brine will foam and ooze up.

Pour the brine to cover the cucumbers completely or they will spoil (this particular fermentation takes place only when there is no oxygen). If you haven't enough brine, make more. Cucumbers float, so to make certain they stay under the brine put a plate on top of them and weight it down with a rock or something heavy.

Place the crock in a warm place for the pickles to ferment. Yeasts do their work best at 65° to 75° fahrenheit. Scum forms where oxygen reaches the brine, and is the beginning of a rotting rather than a fermenting process. Remove the scum that gathers on the top of the crock every day. If you don't, the pickles will spoil. A slotted spoon will work well for this job.

Allow the pickles to ferment for between two and four weeks. The only way to tell if fermentation has progressed far enough is to take out a pickle, slice it, and see if it looks more like a pickle than a cucumber — more translucent than opaque. You might taste it also.

When the pickles are the way you want them (some people like them young and light, some old and dark) and if you can't eat them all quickly, pick them out of the brine and pack them into clean quart jars. Strain the brine and boil it again before you pour it on the pickles. They will keep safely in the refrigerator for a month.

# Sweet Pickled Everything

Another way to pickle vegetables is to boil them in a vinegar and sugar solution. Both vinegar and sugar, like acid and salt, have preserving qualities that discourage decay. Every recipe for pickling vegetables is a little different. If you look up a recipe for cauliflower pickles, you'll see the amounts of sugar and vinegar are different than the recipe for carrot pickles or onion pickles, etc. This is confusing. We have devised a recipe that, though possibly not perfect for everything, is good enough for just about anything.

## Preparing The Vegetables

**You need: carrots, cauliflower, string beans, wax beans, tiny onions, onion slices, hot red peppers, sweet peppers, cucumbers, green cherry tomatoes, or beets (if you don't mind the whole mixture turning red)**
**bowl**
**salt water — three-quarters cup salt to one quart water**
**collander**

Select the vegetables you want to use. Clean and cut them into bite-sized pieces. Put them all in a bowl together and cover with salt water. Let them stand overnight. Rinse the vegetables in a collander with plenty of cold water.

## Making The Syrup

**You need: saucepan**
**2 cups sugar**
**2 cups cider vinegar**
**cinnamon stick, cloves, commercial pickling spices (come already mixed)**

Boil the sugar and vinegar together in a saucepan. The mixture will become syrupy after awhile. If you like spices, add a cinnamon stick and a couple of cloves. You can use commercial pickling spices, too, or make a mixture yourself from white or black pepper, whole allspice, mustard seed, bay leaf, turmeric and dried hot peppers.

## Cleaning The Jars

**You need: jelly jars with tight-fitting screw lids or screw-top Ball or Mason jars**

Wash the jars under very hot tap water with soap. Make sure they are really clean and well rinsed. Most likely you won't be keeping these sweet pickles for a long time and so you won't have to sterilize the jars. Just keep the finished product in the refrigerator and eat it as soon as possible.

## Pickling The Vegetables

Cooking the vegetables can be tricky. Each kind of vegetable has a different cooking time, so you can't just throw the vegetables into the syrup together. Cook one kind of vegetable at a time. Pickled vegetables are supposed to be crisp, so you have to be careful to cook the pieces only until you can get a sharp kitchen fork into them — not until they are soft.

Now take one of the washed jars. Try not to

touch the rim or inside of the jar with your hands. Remove the vegetables from the syrup with a slotted spoon, and put them right into the jar. You can mix the vegetables if you want. Pour boiling syrup over the vegetables in each jar to within one half inch of the top, and seal the lid of each by screwing it on before you fill the next jar. If you're short of syrup, make another batch so all the jars can be filled.

# Sauerkraut

Sauerkraut or kraut for short is nothing more than cabbage and salt mixed together and left to ferment.

You need: knife
head of cabbage
cutting board
large bowl
coarse Kosher or pickling salt, which does not contain iodine
rock or weight
plate or plastic wrap to cover bowl

Cut the cabbage into quarters and remove the solid white center core. Shred the cabbage by slicing it thin with a sharp knife on a cutting board.

Arrange a layer of shredded cabbage in the bowl and sprinkle it with salt. Keep adding layers of cabbage and sprinkling them with salt until all the cabbage is in the bowl. Wash the rock, and put it on top of the cabbage to weight it down. Then cover the bowl with the plate or some plastic wrap.

Leave the bowl out at room temperature for about one week. Then uncover and taste. It should taste like raw sauerkraut, but if it seems too cabbagy allow it to ferment a little longer.

**To Cook Sauerkraut**

You can eat sauerkraut raw, but it tastes better cooked.

You need: 2 cups raw sauerkraut
collander or strainer
1 cup beef broth or 1 bouillon cube dissolved in 1 cup of hot water
½ cup cider or peeled apple
knife
1 sliced onion
caraway seeds (if you like them)
1 potato peeled and sliced to thicken kraut
pepper

**sausages or frankfurters or
pork bits (optional)**

Drain the sauerkraut in a collander and put it in a big pot. Add some beef broth or a diluted bouillon cube, cider if you have it, or a peeled apple, cored and cut up, a sliced onion, and caraway seeds if you like them. Add the sliced potato if you prefer the sauerkraut thick instead of runny. Cook it over low heat for about one hour. It only needs to get tender. You won't need to add salt, but you might like a little pepper.

Any kind of sausages — hot or sweet Italian, regular breakfast, hot dogs, knackwurst, or even leftover pork bits — can be cooked right with the sauerkraut for the last twenty minutes. The meat makes the sauerkraut taste better, and the kraut makes the meat taste better.

# Yogurt

Making yogurt is not difficult, but you must have a yogurt culture for a starter. Commercial yogurt can be used.

**You need: quart of milk
biggest pot you have
⅓ container of plain yogurt
without preservatives or**

**other additives
spoon
empty jars
bath towel
fruit or jam (optional)**

Pour the milk into the pot and bring it almost to a boil over medium heat. The pot should be big because milk boils over very quickly and is a mess to clean up. Keep the flame low after the milk is heated and it won't foam up. Let it simmer (See introduction) for fifteen minutes.

Cool the milk until it's lukewarm — just a little warmer than your finger. Stir in the plain yogurt. Pour the mixture into jelly, peanut butter, pickle, or mayonnaise jars which have been cleaned thoroughly. Close them tightly. Rinse the pot and put the filled jars into it. Fill the pot to the necks of the jars with the hottest water you can get out of your tap. Wrap the pot in a bathtowel to keep it warm.

Now wait five hours. When that much time has passed, you should have yogurt in the jars. Open one and check. If it's not runny, it's yogurt. Chill it in the refrigerator for about an hour and then it's ready to eat plain or with canned fruits or jam. But don't eat it all — save one-third cup to use as your starter for the next batch. That way you won't have to buy yogurt ever again.

# Cottage Cheese

Cottage cheese was probably called cottage cheese because it's so easy to make that any ordinary person living in any ordinary cottage could make it. It's made from soured milk, and in the days before refrigerators, there was plenty of soured milk. Milk still sours these days if you leave it out of the refrigerator for a day.

**You need: soured milk**
**saucepan**
**scissors**
**cheesecloth**
**collander or strainer**
**bowl**
**salt and pepper**

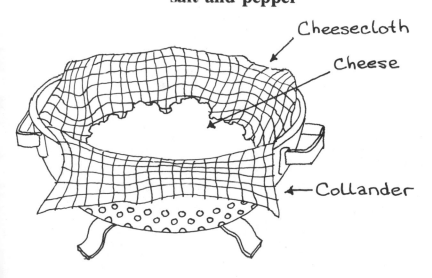

Heat the soured milk slowly in a saucepan until the whey, a thin liquid, rises to the top. This should happen when the milk reaches boiling temperature. Pour off the whey so only the curd is left. (Now you know what Miss Muffat was eating.)

Cut a big square of cheesecloth (now you know why cheesecloth is called cheesecloth), line a large collander or strainer with it, and place it in the kitchen sink. Put the curd in the cheesecloth, bring the edges of the cloth over the top of the curd so it's covered, and leave it to drain for six hours. Then, dump the curd into a bowl and break it up into large or small curd cottage cheese. Eat it fresh with salt and pepper.

# Dried Apples

The pale dried apple rings you may have bought in stores are bleached that whitish color. The dried apple rings you make will be brown but still taste just as good.

**You need: apples**
**knife**
**string and hooks or nails**

Start with fresh, firm apples which are not mealy. Apples picked in the fall are the best. Peel, core and then slice them into rings about

one-quarter-inch thick. String them as shown in the photograph. Tie both ends of the string horizontally to a couple of nails or hooks. Spread the apple rings so none of them touch. They can be dried outdoors if they are kept out of the sun and away from insects. They can be dried indoors too if the place you hang them is reasonably well ventilated. Leave to dry for about two weeks. Then enjoy them as a snack.

# Candy Apples

This recipe is for a dozen small apples; if they are too big, the amount of candy coating this recipe makes won't be enough to cover them all.

**You need: butter for greasing**
**cookie sheet**

12 small apples
12 popsicle sticks or twigs
1 cup sugar
1 cup corn syrup
vegetable dye (optional)

Butter a cookie sheet large enough to hold all twelve apples. Put the sticks into the stem ends of the apples. Boil the sugar and corn syrup together, stirring only until the sugar melts. When a few drops poured into cold water becomes brittle right away it has been boiled enough. Turn off the heat. Dip the apples into the syrup, one at a time, holding them by their sticks. Place each apple on the cookie sheet, with its stick in the air. If the syrup hardens, heat it for a minute before you dip the next apple.

If you wonder why the candy apples you buy at fairs and circuses are red, vegetable dye was probably added to the syrup. You could try it. For a change, why not try to make the apples blue.

# Pink Applesauce

There is no fantastic trick to making pink applesauce — just use apples with red skins and don't peel them. The red pigment in the skins colors the sauce.

95

**You need: knife**
**apples with red skins**
**large pot**
**sugar (1 tablespoon for each**
**apple makes a sweet sauce)**
**spices like ground cloves,**
**nutmeg, mace, cinnamon,**
**allspice**
**food mill**

**heavy cream or sour cream**
**(optional)**

Cut the apples, but you don't need to peel or core them.

Spill the apples into a large pot, and sprinkle the sugar on them. Add more sugar when the apples get mushy if you think there isn't enough. Cover the pot and heat over a very low flame. You don't need any water, because the apples release water as they soften. Stir them frequently so they don't stick and burn. Sugar, by the way, makes the sauce velvety and glossy.

You can add the seasonings as soon as the apples are mushy enough to taste. Try only a little at first because spices like cloves and cinnamon can taste awfully strong awfully fast.

Now uncover the pot so some of the water in it evaporates as the apples cook. Don't forget to stir. The applesauce is done when it loses that watery look, and plops as it boils. Apples vary in how much water they contain so it can take from half an hour to an hour before yours are ready.

Now comes the nasty part: you have to put the sauce through a food mill to get rid of pits, stems and skin. It's work. The applesauce is worth it though — it's not like anything that came out of a can. For a real treat, eat it with heavy cream. Sour cream is terrific too.

# Apple Butter

**You need:** **applesauce**
**cloves, cinnamon or other**
    **spices**
**butter**

To make applesauce into apple butter, put the strained sauce back in the pot and cook it over a very low flame for a while longer. Add more spices, particularly cloves and cinnamon, but don't forget to taste as you add. When it becomes dark and thick, it's apple butter. Mix in some butter (approximately one pat for each cup of apple butter), while the apple butter is warm enough to melt it. Then spread it on bread. Store leftover applebutter in the refrigerator.

What might also work — but we haven't tried it yet — is to start with commercial applesauce and see if you can make apple butter from that. It might work fine, but you will most likely have to add sugar as well as the spices.

# Nut Butter

Peanut butter is nothing more than crushed peanuts. Some commercial brands add preservatives to keep it fresher longer but you don't need to if you eat yours within a few days. (It keeps a few weeks in the

A chopping bowl is good for crushing nuts. Use a rock (harder work) or a wooden pounder. A mortar and pestle is easier to use.

refrigerator.) Other nuts make wonderful butters too. Try almonds, cashews, walnuts, hazelnuts, peanuts, or pecans. Raw cashews, found in most health food stores make a particularly sweet and good nut butter. Canned nuts can also be used. Almonds usually come with their skins on and will have to be blanched. To blanch nuts, put them in boiling water for a few minutes, then drain them. Slip off their skins by pinching them between your fingers. Salted cocktail nuts will make a saltier butter of course and nuts in their shells are naturally more work.

**You need: nuts**
**bowl**
**pounder, rock, mortar and**
**pestle, or blender**

Shell and blanch the nuts to get off their skins if necessary. Now put them in the bowl and pound and pound. Or put them in the blender and let it do the work. After a while, you will have nut butter.

# Sweet Butter

You wouldn't want to make butter more than once or twice because it's really awfully expensive. But it proves that real fresh butter — the way people used to eat it — is quite different from what you buy in bars.

**You need: ½ pint heavy cream**
**bowl**
**egg beater or electric mixer**
**fine mesh strainer**
**salt (optional)**

Pour the heavy cream into a bowl and beat it with the egg beater or with the electric mixer. First it will become thick and then turn to whipped cream. Keep beating. The whipped cream will get thicker and, in only a minute or so more, form lumps and separate. The pale yellow lumps are butter. The liquid left after the butter has formed is fresh buttermilk and should not be thrown away. Strain the mixture through a fine mesh strainer to collect the butter. Add salt if you like, but genuine butter lovers don't.

# Taffy Pull

Taffy is an old-fashioned candy that has probably been popular as much because of the fun of making it as the taste. People used to invite friends over for a taffy-pull party.

**You need: 2 cups water**
**2 cups sugar**
**4 tablespoons butter**
**2 teaspoons cream of tartar**

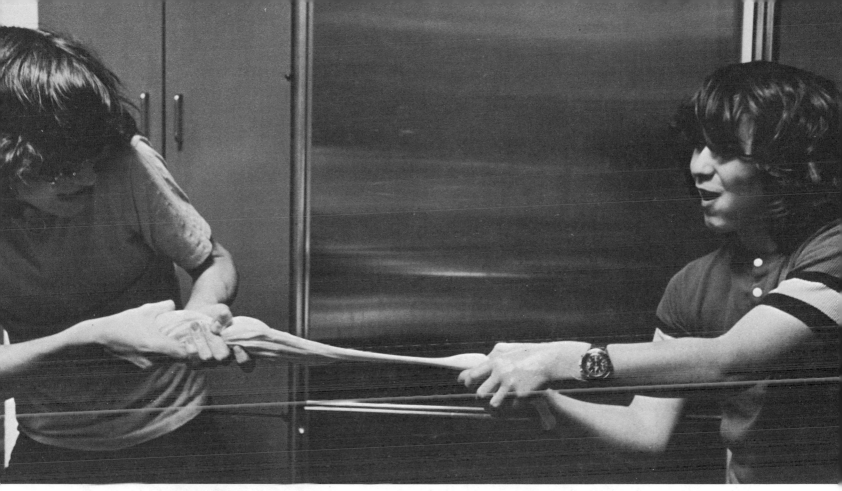

**saucepan**
**vanilla, orange, lemon,**
   **almond, peppermint, or**
   **other flavoring**
**buttered pan**
**friend, brother, or sister**
**waxed paper**
**scissors**

Boil everything except the flavoring (waxed paper and scissors and the friend, of course) in a saucepan until when you drop a bit of the candy into cold water, it turns brittle right away. (If you use a candy thermometer, it should read 268°.) Stir in a teaspoon of vanilla, or half that amount of another flavoring.

Pour the mixture into a buttered pan so it can cool down for a while. As soon as you can handle it without saying ouch (this does *not* mean cool — it means as hot as you can stand it), butter your hands. Pick up the candy, pull it quickly, put it back together, pull it again,

99

and keep going until it gets white and shiny. If you are doing it with someone else, you pull the candy away from one another, then walk quickly back together to double up the rope. Pull again. When it looks like taffy and is getting cool, stretch it out in ropes on waxed paper and cut it into short lengths with scissors before it gets too hard.

# Burnt Berry Jelly

No matter how you cook berries, sugar, and water the results will taste good. If the mixture jells after you follow these instructions, you have jelly. If it doesn't, you can use the mixture as ice cream sauce, pancake syrup or jam. You can't lose.

Whether you end up with jelly or syrup depends on the fruit you use. Cooked fruit jells because it contains pectin, and some kinds of fruits have more pectin than others. We found that wild gooseberries and currants cooked together would jell, but gooseberries alone wouldn't. No one liked the gooseberries anyway. Blueberries and blackberries made syrup or sauce. Berries make a thicker sauce if you leave out the water. Wild quinces and rose hips made jelly. So did crabapples. If you have a crabapple tree around, you can add these little apples to any other kind of fruit

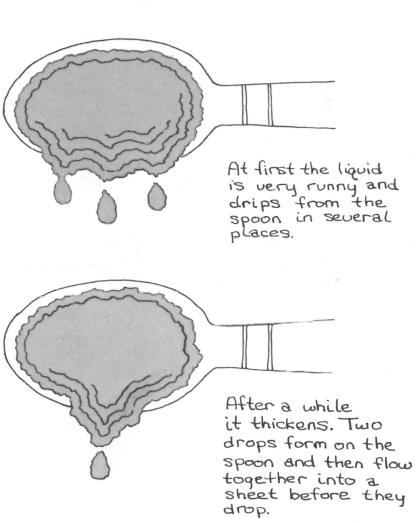

At first the liquid is very runny and drips from the spoon in several places.

After a while it thickens. Two drops form on the spoon and then flow together into a sheet before they drop.

101

Gooseberries

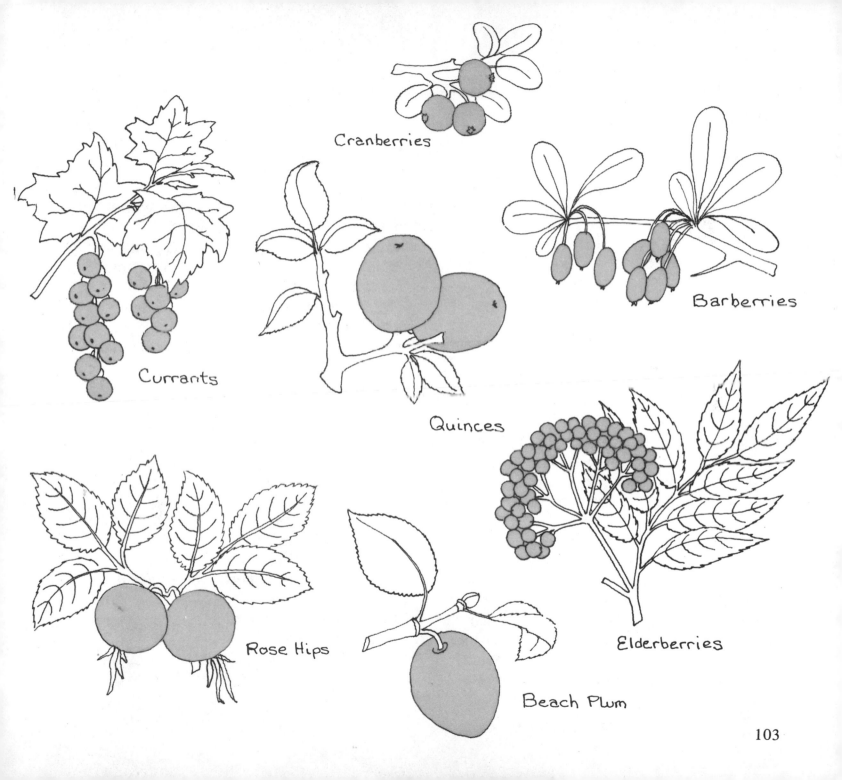

Cranberries

Currants

Quinces

Barberries

Rose Hips

Beach Plum

Elderberries

103

and get the mixture to jell without hurting the flavor. If the mixture doesn't taste sweet enough, add sugar.

**You need: 1 measure of berries or fruits**
**like crabapples, quinces,**
**beach plums, or rose hips**
**1 measure water**
**1 measure sugar**
**large pot**
**Ball or Mason jars**
**strainer (optional)**

The reason for saying ''measure'' instead of cup is because when you buy or pick wild berries, you can end up with anything from a canful to a pailful or more. If you only have an orange juice can of berries, then that's how much water and sugar to use too. If you've collected a full pail of berries then use that much sugar and that much water.

Put the fruit, water and sugar into a big pot that is much too large for them. That leaves enough room for the syrup to boil up without boiling over. Put it on the stove over medium heat only and bring to a boil. Boil until when you stick a spoon into it and lift the spoon out again, the mixture is thick enough so that the two drops that form on it flow together into a sheet and then drop off. This takes more than a quarter of an hour and often as long as half an hour.

When the mixture is that thick, take it off the stove and pour it into hot Ball or Mason jelly jars. Heat the jars by running very hot water over them in a large pot. Don't use glasses — they will break from the sudden heat.

If you just want syrup or jelly without any pieces of fruit, pour the mixture through a strainer. Syrup or jelly will keep in the refrigerator, but may ferment or get moldy at room temperature.

But why, you ask, is this called *burnt* berry jelly? Well, when we make it, we often forget to stir it enough and it burns at the bottom of the pot. It still tastes fine.

# Brain Food

If you sometimes feel a yearning for a candy bar before a test, there may be a reason. The brain uses more sugar than any other part of your body, and there are those who believe that a modest supply of sugar before a test can boost your brain's energy for a short period of time. No one is sure how but it seems your body lets you know when it needs a quick supply of sugar.

However, to burn up the extra calories you get in a candy bar you would have to bend and touch your toes 500 times. So, a better solution might be to eat a hamburger or a cheeseburger with ketchup. The ketchup has sufficient sugar in it for fast energy, and the protein from the cheese and meat will supply your body with long-term energy.

# Cure For Hiccups

No one is sure why this works, but it does. When you can't get rid of hiccups, eat a spoonful of granulated sugar. The hiccups will stop as soon as the sugar is in your mouth, even before you swallow it.

# Two Ways To Stop Burns From Hurting

Long ago people used to keep an aloe plant growing on their kitchen windowsills to treat burns. Herb nurseries are the most likely place to find an aloe now. Should you have an aloe plant in your kitchen and you happen to get a burn, squeeze the leaves to get the juice, then wipe the juice on the burn. Aloe juice is a

An aloe plant

common ingredient in sunburn ointments.

Today most people have baking soda in the kitchen. If you get a burn, mix regular baking soda with water to make a thin paste. Spoon the paste liberally onto the burn. It will relieve most of the pain right away. When it starts to hurt again, rinse off the first paste, which is probably a little dry, and put more on.

# Hint For Migraine Headache Sufferers

People who get migraines can usually feel them coming on before their heads really hurt. This is the time to try to forestall the migraine with caffeine, a substance found in coffee.

**You need: very strong coffee**

Make (or ask an adult to make) a cup of very strong coffee and then drink it. This remedy is often prescribed for children who have migraines because most of the drugs that help adults are too strong for children. Caffeine will help adults too if they drink the coffee soon enough.

# Cure For Bee Stings

Keep meat tenderizer in the kitchen. If you get stung, rub some tenderizer onto the sting right away. Meat tenderizer is really an enzyme that digests protein. You may not like what it does to your meat, but it's wonderful for countering bee venom. The pain stops right away. However, if you don't use it immediately, it won't work because the venom will have already spread too far from the site of the sting for the tenderizer to reach it.

It might be a good idea to carry some tenderizer with you on picnics and other outings where there may be bees.

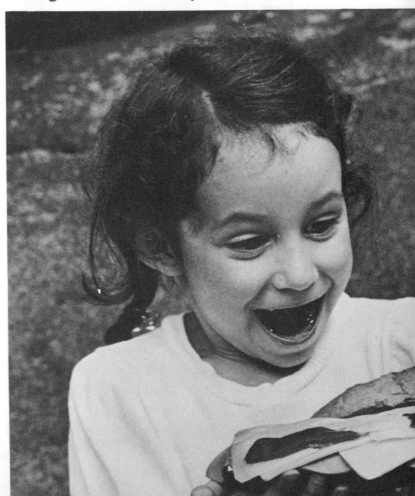

# The Single Sandwich Picnic

Sick of sog sandwiches? Tired of drip pickles? Fed up with shoving sloppy stuff into sticky bags? Here at last is the single sandwich picnic. There's only one catch: everyone in your family has to eat the same things. So step number one is to get your family to agree on one list of ingredients for the sandwich.

**You need: knife**
**one very long loaf of Italian bread**

spreads such as mayonnaise,
mustard, butter
extras such as raw onion,
coleslaw, olives, pimentos,
pickles
meats such as boiled ham,
liverwurst, salami, turkey,
bologna
cheeses such as American,
muenster, Swiss

Slice the whole loaf lengthwise. Spread the bottom half with mayonnaise, mustard, butter, or all three. Lay on the extras first — the olives, pickles, coleslaw. The spread will keep them in the sandwich. Now lay on the meats and cheeses, and finally the top half of the bread. Wrap the whole thing up in a piece of foil, or waxed paper if you're not going to keep it too long. Bring a knife with you. When you get to the picnic, slice the one sandwich into smaller sandwiches.

# Mixed-Up Sardines

Mixed-up sardines are swell on toast or crackers, and take only a few minutes to make.

You need: hard-boiled egg
can of sardines
bowl
knife
mayonnaise, worcestershire
sauce, hot pepper or hot
sauce, lemon juice or
vinegar, ketchup, or other
flavorings
toast or crackers

First hard-boil an egg (see introduction) and open a can of sardines. Drain the oil or liquid from the sardines and shell the egg (see introduction). Put them both in a bowl and chop them up together. You can do this with a plain table knife if you don't have a special chopper. Add the flavorings to suit your own taste.

By this time, the mixture may not taste much like sardines or egg but it's certainly good. Spread the final results on toast or crackers.

# Deviled Eggs

Nothing quite pleases your parents as much as surprising them with a luxury lunch or providing them with canapes for cocktails. You'll enjoy it more if what you make is something you love to eat also. Since deviled

eggs look elegant (if you haven't been too sloppy), and are usually loved by both adults and kids, they're a good way to make both you and the grownups happy.

**You need:** **one hard-boiled egg per person (see introduction)**
**knife**
**bowl**
**fork**
**mayonnaise**
**lemon juice**
**mustard**
**salt and pepper**
**caper, pickle, olive, or other garnish**

Shell the eggs (see introduction) and cut them in half lengthwise. Remove the yolks, put them in a bowl and mash them up with a fork. Add enough mayonnaise to make the mixture soft and creamy and enough lemon juice to give it some snap. Start small — you can always add more of either. Add a bit of prepared mustard or a pinch or so of dry (hot!) mustard and sprinkle on some salt and pepper. Taste it. If it's too bland, try to decide if more lemon juice, mayonnaise, mustard, or pepper would help, and add more of any of them. You could also add worcestershire sauce if you want.

When the mixture tastes good, and before you've eaten too much of it, stuff a heaping teaspoon in each of the egg whites. To make the deviled eggs more like canapes and less like a picnic lunch, decorate each egg half with a caper, pickle slice, pinch of paprika, olive slice, parsley sprig, or a small piece of anchovy.

# Bone Soup

Did you know that bones can make a wonderful broth? They do and the broth tastes good enough to eat alone or, if you want, you can add lots of other things.

**You need:** **marrow bones (one whole beef shin bone cut up by the butcher should make a quart of broth or more)**
**big pot**
**salt and pepper**
**macaroni, dried beans, carrots, onions, any herbs that smell right to you, pepper, rice, string beans, cauliflower, tomatoes, beets, green or red pepper, spinach, watercress, etc. (optionals)**
**grated cheese**
**toast**

Put the marrow bones in a big pot filled with water and bring it to a boil over a medium flame. Don't cover the pot. Lower the flame so that the water is barely boiling and skim off any scum that forms. After about three and a half hours add some salt and taste the broth. If it tastes like salty water, you haven't cooked the bones long enough or you haven't used enough of them. If it tastes good, take out the bones and save the broth.

Now you can either eat the soup as it is or add any other ingredients you'd like. If you want to use dried beans, they will take several hours to cook. All the other ingredients take only about twenty minutes.

If you like, sprinkle grated cheese on top, or add a piece of toast which will float.

# Marrow Toast

Marrow is the tasty soft substance found in the middle of hollow bones. Most people today seem to have forgotten how good it is to eat. Marrow bones, usually a cow or calf's shin bone, used to be free at the butcher's. Although some stores now charge for them, the price is still pretty low. You may have to ask the butcher to cut some marrow bones specially for you.

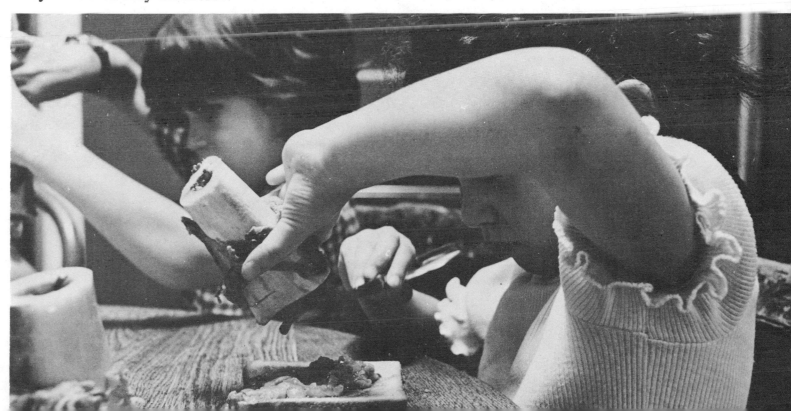

**You need:** **marrow bones**
**large pot**
**kitchen spoon**
**bread**
**knife**
**salt and pepper**

Put the marrow bones in a pot with a little water. Boil them over a medium flame until the marrow is soft. This won't take more than fifteen or twenty minutes. Take the bones out of the water with a spoon and let them cool until you can handle them.

While the bones are cooling, toast some bread. Use a knife to scoop out the marrow while it is still warm and spread it on the toast. Sprinkle a little salt and pepper on if you like. Marrow not only tastes good, it is also very nourishing.

# Homemade Pasta

Fresh pasta is delicious and tastes much nicer than the kind you buy in the supermarket. You can make it easily from only two ingredients.

**You need:** **3 cups flour**
**4 eggs**
**rolling pin**
**knife**
**large pot**

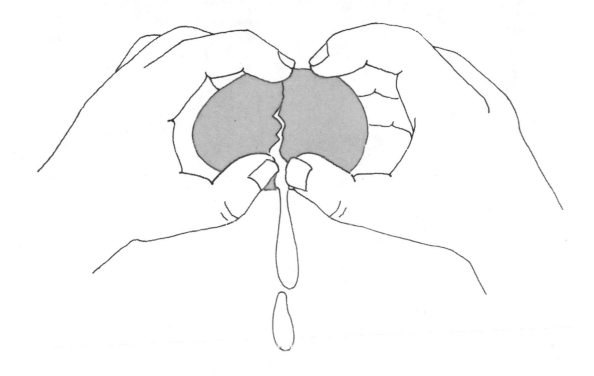

Heap the flour into a hill on a smooth-topped table or counter. Make a well in the middle of the hill, and break the eggs into it. Mix them into the flour with your hands. Keep working the mixture until you have a stiff, tough, rubbery dough. That what pasta dough is supposed to be like.

Of course, that is also the problem with pasta dough. It's so tough and rubbery that it's very hard to roll. So scrape off any dough stuck to the surface with a spatula, sprinkle flour on the table or counter, divide the dough into three chunks, and roll out each one separately. It gets easier as it gets thinner. Make the sheet as thin as you can and let it dry for about ten minutes uncovered. Then sprinkle some flour on the sheet of dough so it won't stick to itself and roll it up.

Slice the roll into strips as thick as you want your noodles to be. Lasagna is about two inches wide, other noodles are narrower. Unroll each slice for your noodles. If you just can't take the rolling, snip off bits of dough to cook instead. You can call it "lumperoni."

Boil the fresh pasta in a large pot of boiling water the same as you would for spaghetti. It cooks much more quickly than commercial pasta, so check it often.

You can also dry noodles to use some other time. But if you want to dry them, you have to hang them someplace where they can rest undisturbed for a few days. And try to do it when the weather's dry, or during the winter when the heat is on. When the pasta is hard, break it up if it's too long and store it in jars until needed.

# Pick-A-Pasta

Pasta of any shape is one of the easiest things to cook.

**You need:** **large pot**
**pasta (choose one with an interesting shape)**
**collander or strainer**
**for hot pasta: melted butter, margarine, or olive oil**
**for cold pasta: mayonnaise, lemon juice, or vinegar**
**flavorings or optional ingredients: grated cheese or American cheese cut up;**
**walnuts; crushed garlic; pimentos; bologna or leftover meats; tuna fish or anchovies; fresh tomato; canned kidney beans or chick peas; pickles or relish; herbs like parsley, chives, oregano, sage, thyme, basil, or savory**

Fill a large pot two-thirds full of water and bring it to a boil over a medium flame. Throw in the pasta (half a box of elbow macaroni is enough for two people). Stir it around a little so the pasta doesn't stick together, and turn the heat lower if the water foams up and spills all over the stove. Stir it a few more times as it cooks. The pasta should seem soft enough to eat in only about ten minutes. Now pour the whole potful, water and all, into a large collander or strainer in the sink, and then rinse the pasta under very hot tap water so it's not too sticky.

Once you have cooked your pasta, you can eat it hot or cold in a bunch of different ways. The principle is to first add something that will prevent the pasta from sticking together: If you eat it hot, add melted butter, margarine, or olive oil; if you eat it cold, mayonnaise, and maybe some lemon juice or vinegar (plus salt and pepper). Then experiment with flavor by adding any or several of the optional ingredients.

If you want to make a fancy dinner out of the pasta, choose a number of things you like and put them in bowls on the table. Then everyone can sprinkle and mix what they like on their own pasta.

# Drink Experiments

Since experiments in drinking wouldn't be experimental if you had recipes, you must think up your own drinks. Use our examples as suggestions. For instance, if your parents say you should eat more eggs because they are full of protein, the news is that a raw egg in any drink doesn't change the flavor much one way or another. For a second instance, if you like orange juice but hate milk, orange juice and milk, half and half, shaken up with some extra sugar tastes like melted orange popsicles. And the milk does not curdle like everyone says it will. Another for instance: if there's only one soda left, and everyone is willing to kill to get it, shake it up with milk and sugar and share it nicely.

Then there's fruit: ripe bananas and most canned fruits mixed up with soda, milk or orange juice in a blender are luscious. So are

jams. So are syrups. And no one has to tell you about milkshakes made with ice cream. Some people love to add malt to drinks. If you do, you can usually buy it in a health food store. If you have any mint growing around you, stick a snip of it into almost any blender drink. Try molasses. Try honey. Don't forget lemon juice and lemon rind. And what's wrong in mixing tea with other things? Have you ever thought of peanut butter? In a drink? Almond extract is absolutely wonderful. Peppermint extract maybe, and good old vanilla. By all means sprinkle cinnamon, mace, allspice and nutmeg (liberally.) And if your thirst is up and you wonder which of these marvelous concoctions the boy is drinking in the photograph, it's plain old eggnog. One egg, a glass of milk, vanilla, nutmeg and sugar. Don't envy him though — he had to drink a whole quart of it to get this photograph.

# Dips And Things To Dip With

A dip is any soft, tasty stuff you can scoop up onto a harder bit of food and pop into your mouth. Our basic dip is cream cheese softened with cream, milk or sour cream.

**You need:** cream cheese
milk, sour cream, or cream
flavorings: worchestershire sauce; horseradish; garlic or garlic salt; mustard; soy sauce; dill, chives parsley, basil, or other herbs; curry powder; paprika, ginger, or other spices
things to mix into the dip (chop them first): olives; nuts; anchovies; pickles (or relish); capers; deviled ham; cooked clams; cooked bacon; salami; pimentos; tuna fish; blue-mold cheeses; scallions or Bermuda onion
things to dip with: carrot sticks, cauliflower, celery, string beans, or other fresh raw vegetables; crackers, toast or melba toast; potato chips; fingers

Let the cream cheese warm to room temperature before you start. When you add the milk, sour cream, or cream to make it softer, add only a little at a time, mixing with a spoon, so it stays smooth. Judge for yourself

117

how soft you want the dip to be.

What you put into a dip depends on your own tastes but the principle is that the strong taste of what you add is softened by the taste of the cream cheese. So if you don't like anchovies because they taste so strong you might love anchovy dip because it tastes milder.

# Cheese Rabbit

"Cheese rabbit" is a name we have devised ourselves for a dish which is neither Welsh rabbit nor cheese fondue. It is not fondue because fondue usually requires wine. It is not Welsh rabbit because Welsh rabbit, though easy to make, is eaten with knives and forks and isn't as much fun as fondue. This dish is more or less a "rabbit" you eat by dipping bread into it as though it were fondue.

**You need: double boiler or pot with a**
**bowl that fits inside it**
**without slipping**
**Swiss, American, or gruyere**
**cheese**
**milk**
**worchestershire sauce, hot**
**sauce, barbeque sauce,**
**ketchup, mustard, garlic,**

black pepper, or other
seasoning
crusty bread (French or
Italian) or cut up toast

Boil water in the bottom of a double boiler. If you don't have one, use a large pot and a bowl which will fit into it. Break or cut up the cheese and put it in the top of the double boiler or bowl. Place the top pot into the bottom one. The cheese will soon begin to melt. As it gets soft, stir in a little milk until it gets as thick or as thin and gooey as you like. Add whatever flavorings appeal to you, tasting as you go along so you don't overdo it. When the cheese rabbit tastes delicious and is a smooth consistency, move the whole double boiler onto the table. The hot water will keep the rabbit soft enough to eat.

Eat this by dipping chunks of bread or bits of toast into the rabbit and popping them into your mouth.

# Fried Cheese Sandwiches

We think cheese sandwiches taste best when they are fried in a frying pan. The browned butter is the reason this kind of cheese

119

sandwich is so much better than regular toasted cheese.

**You need:** **2 slices of bread**
**2 slices of American cheese**
**2 pats of butter**
**frying pan**
**spatula**

Take the bread slices and put the American cheese between them. Melt a pat of butter in a frying pan, then put the sandwich in. Keep the pan on a low heat. When the bread is brown on one side, lift the sandwich with a spatula, add another pat of butter and turn the sandwich over. When the second side is brown, the cheese should be gooey. If it isn't, you had the heat too high so the cheese didn't get a chance to melt before the bread got brown.

Try making the same sandwich with cream cheese. When it melts it tastes quite different then cold cream cheese.

# Gashouse Special

I'm forced to include gashouse specials in this book because my husband insists he invented them. Sometimes he says his Uncle Jack invented them. Gashouse specials are the only thing he knows how to cook.

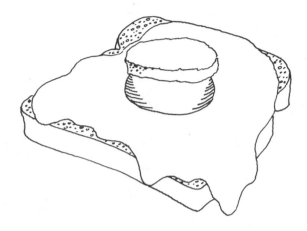

**You need:** **toast**
**cookie cutter (optional)**
**butter**
**frying pan with lid**
**egg**
**ketchup**

Toast a slice of bread. Tear a hole in the middle with your fingers or cut a circle with a cookie cutter and save the round piece. Melt a pat of butter in a frying pan, put the toast in it, and break an egg into the hole. Keep it on a low heat and cover the pan. When the white of the egg turns white, the gashouse special is done. Put the round piece of toast over the yolk as a sort of cap. This is good with ketchup.

# Cinnamon Toast

The best way to have all the cinnamon toast you want to eat, when you want to eat it, is to prepare a mixture of cinnamon, sugar, and butter and keep it in the refrigerator.

**You need:** **½ pound butter or margarine**
**bowl**
**1 cup granulated sugar**
**fork**
**2 tablespoons ground**
  **cinnamon**
**toast**

Leave a half pound of butter or margarine out until it's really soft. In a bowl, mix the granulated sugar and the cinnamon into the soft butter with a fork. When this mixture is well blended, put it into a plastic container (an empty margarine tub with a lid is good for this) and return it to the refrigerator.

Now any time you want cinnamon toast fast, all you have to do is spread the mixture on toast and stick it under a low broiler flame for a minute until the top bubbles. When it bubbles, it means the sugar is melting. The butter will soak into the toast and the sugar will form a crunchy candy coating.

# French Pancakes

The French word for pancakes is crêpes, and crêpes usually are considered something you order in a restaurant where a trained chef is in charge of the mysteries. The only mystery about these pancakes is how anyone could ever have made them seem mysterious. They're a cinch.

**You need:** **1 cup flour**
**½ teaspoon salt**
**bowl**
**1 cup milk (or more if your**
  **pancakes come out too thick)**
**2 eggs**
**egg beater or whisk**
**pitcher**
**small frying pan**
**butter or margarine for**
  **cooking**

Put the flour and salt in a bowl, stir in the milk, drop in the eggs and beat up the mixture with an egg beater or a whisk until it's smooth. It should be the consistency of a runny milkshake. Put the batter in a pitcher so you can pour it into the pan.

You cook the pancakes one at a time in a small frying pan. Grease the pan with a few

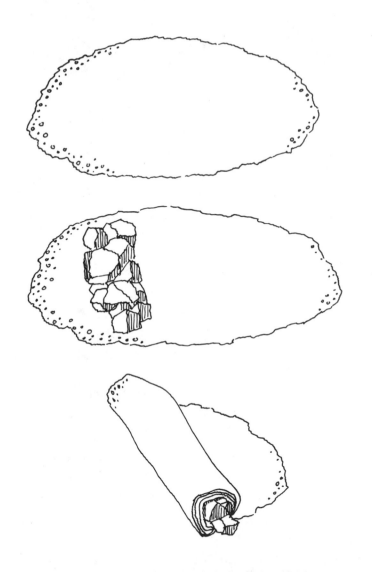

completely covers the bottom in a very thin layer. If the batter makes a thick clumsy pancake, just add some more milk to it to thin it down.

When the edges of the pancake get dry and lacy-looking, turn it over with a fork or a spatula to cook on the other side. They cook very quickly. The first side will be golden in color but the second side will stay pale. Add a little oil, butter, or margarine each time you cook a pancake.

Sometimes part of the first pancake will stick on the pan. Usually scraping the pan afterwards will prevent the others from sticking.

To eat crêpes, put your favorite jelly in the middle of the pale side and roll it up so the golden side shows.

If you've made more batter than you want to cook right now, you can keep it in the refrigerator and cook another snack from it tomorrow.

# Unstuffed Stuffing

Stuffing fiends don't need to wait for Thanksgiving. And stuffing doesn't have to be stuffed into a bird and roasted to be a good snack.

drops of cooking oil or a tiny dab of butter or margarine. Heat it over medium heat. Now comes the fun. Pour in a little of the batter, only a few tablespoonsful. Tilt the pan to one side and then the other so the batter

**You need:** knife
4 slices bread
bowl
2 pats butter
frying pan
small onion
sage, rosemary, thyme,
  savory or other herbs
salt and pepper

Cut as much bread as you think you can eat (four slices, perhaps) into cubes — the size of the cubes doesn't matter much. Put the cubes into a bowl. Melt a pat of butter for every two slices of bread or one half pat for every slice in a frying pan. Slice an onion into the melted butter and cook it until the onion looks soft and glassy. If you like the taste of browned onion, turn up the heat and cook the onion until it is brown and crispy. Mix the butter and onion gradually into the cubes of bread, tossing the cubes with a fork. Let your own nose and tongue tell you how much of each herb — sage, rosemary, thyme, or savory plus salt and pepper — to add.

And that's it — stuffing!

# Uncooked Cookies

As anyone who has ever scraped the cookie

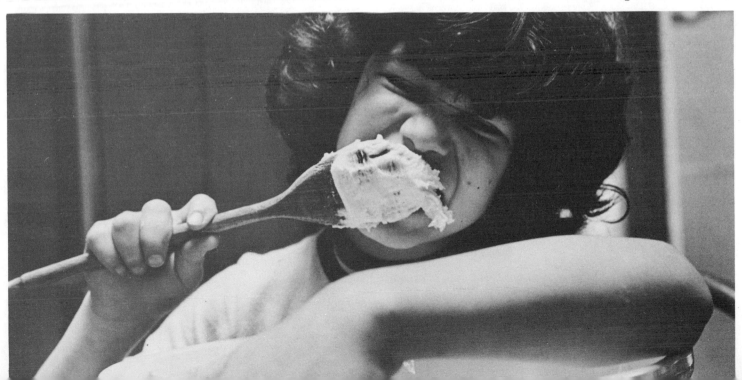

bowl knows, raw cookies are better than cooked cookies. As anyone who has ever been caught helping himself to gobs of dough has been warned, raw cookies will make you sick. However, we have not found that to be true, and this is a good recipe for uncooked cookies. (Take it easy at first — maybe your stomach is different from ours.)

**You need: ½ cup softened butter**
**bowl**
**1 cup sugar**
**1 egg**
**½ teaspoon vanilla, or ¼**
**teaspoon of another flavor**
**extract like orange or**
**almond**
**1½ cups flour**
**salt**
**1 teaspoon baking powder**
**(optional)**

Take the butter out of the refrigerator and leave it in a bowl to get soft. Then stir the sugar, egg, milk, and flavor extract into the softened butter. When that's mixed well, stir in the flour and salt. Eat.

If you really want to bake these cookies, mix a teaspoon of baking powder in with the flour and salt before you add it to the butter mixture. Drop the dough by spoonfuls onto a greased cookie sheet, and bake at 375° for ten minutes or less. They are done when the edges begin to brown.

If you love to cut cookies into fancy shapes, add about another quarter cup of flour to your dough to make it stiffer, chill it in the refrigerator, and then roll the dough out on a floured table, sprinkling flour on the rolling pin as you go along to keep it from sticking. When the rolled dough is a quarter inch thick, that's thin enough to cut and bake but if you can get it thinner the cookies will be crispier.

# Edible Sprouts

Get different kinds of uncooked seeds and beans from a health food store. Do not use beans or seeds that are meant for vegetable gardens, because sometimes they have been treated with chemicals that may be poisonous.

**You need: Mung beans, soy beans, or**
**wheat berries**
**jar**
**cheesecloth**
**rubber band**
**plastic bag**

Sprinkle a single layer of beans in the bottom of a glass jar. You can use one kind, or mix several kinds of beans together. Cover the top of the jar with cheesecloth and secure it with a rubber band. Fill the jar by pouring water through the cheesecloth. Then pour the water out again. Put the plastic bag loosely over the top and keep the jar in a closet or cupboard. Every day, take the bag out, rinse the beans with water through the cheesecloth, pour the water out, and replace the bag.

In a week the beans will have sprouted. Each kind of bean sprout tastes a little different. They are good in bread and butter sandwiches, or just as a snack snipped off with your fingers. If you find one kind of sprout you like best, grow more of them the next time. Chinese bean sprouts are the sprouts of Mung beans.

If you don't want to eat the sprouts, let them continue growing. In another week or so, they will be a beautiful jungle in a jar — the wheat like grass, the beans like small trees. And of course you can see the roots growing as well. It is bothersome to transplant sprouts into pots so if you want to grow bean or grain plants, plant them in soil from the beginning.

# Artichokes

A lot of people seem to be scared of artichokes. Maybe they think that because they look spiny and peculiar, they bite. Other people think you have to be a snob to eat anything so exotic. And some people just don't know where to start eating, and are afraid they might look foolish. An artichoke is only an unopened blossom.

**You need: artichoke**
**knife**
**pot**
**salt**
**fork or kitchen tongs**
**melted butter**
**small pot**
**lemon juice**

Rinse the artichoke. Cut the stem off the artichoke so it's flat on the bottom and stands up straight. Cut about an inch off the top so you won't get your fingers pricked by the small thorns on the top of the leaves. Put the artichoke in a pot with a little water, salt it, cover the pot and let it boil for about a half hour. To tell if it's done, tug at one of the bottom petals with a fork or kitchen tongs. If the petal falls off easily, the artichoke is cooked.

Make a sauce to dip the petals into by melting some butter in a small pot. Keep the flame low so it doesn't burn. Squeeze in some lemon juice. Pour the sauce into a small bowl. Now pull off a bottom petal. Dip it in the

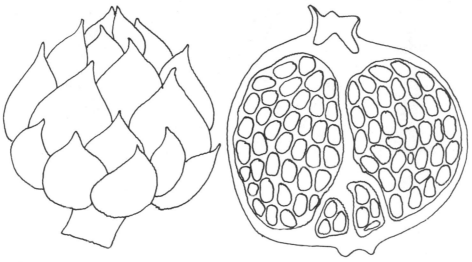

An artichoke, and a pomegranate cut in half.

butter sauce. Hold it in your hand, put its lower half in your mouth, and scrape the soft part off it with your teeth. Throw away the rest of it. Keep eating your way around the artichoke. As you get near the center, the tender portion of the petal becomes larger and larger until you are biting off more than half of each. But just as you are really eager, they get too small and prickly at the top to fuss with.

Now comes the best part of the artichoke — the heart. To get to the heart, lift off the cone of small petals you're not bothering with. Under it will be a layer of fuzzy hairs called the choke. Scrape the choke off with the side of a fork.

The greyish round thing left is the heart. Cut it, dip it in butter, and eat.

Do you notice the sweet taste that is left in your mouth after you have finished eating? Whatever you drink right after an artichoke tastes sweet. Scientists are trying to help dieters by inventing an artichoke-like substance for them to pop in their mouths before drinking a sugarless soft drink giving the illusion that the drink itself is sweet.

# Pomegranates

I've never been sure why pomegranates are such fun to eat. They are not particularly sweet, and they don't have a big flavor, and they certainly don't fill your stomach.

The fruit is made up of small berry-shaped bits, all neatly packed together under the leathery skin. When you bite them, they pop juice. They surprise you. Maybe it's just nice to be surprised by a fruit.

To eat a pomegranate, peel off the skin with the help of a knife, and gnaw and suck the berries inside. The seeds are crunchy and not worth spitting out. Avoid the white pulp which is bitter like the white part of an orange.

# Fried Plantain

Plantains are big, ugly, hard bananas that are only good to eat when they have been cooked. You'll be able to find plantains in stores that sell to Spanish Americans or Jamaicans. They are exotic, good, and cheap.

**You need: plantain**
**knife**
**frying pan**
**oil or butter**
**salt**

When the plantain is ripe, it is quite black, but you don't have to wait for that. We've eaten them while they are still a brownish yellow. Peel them, and slice them either lengthwise into two pieces or diagonally into thick slices. If they're too hard to peel, the fruit is unripe and will be tasteless. Fry them in oil or butter over low heat until they are brown. Drain, salt, and eat them. They taste slightly like a banana, but are more starchy and tangy. Besides snacks, plantains make a swell vegetable with regular dinners.

# The Ultimate Banana Split

Really fantastic banana splits have to be a special family venture, because you probably don't have all the things you need around. The best way is to have *everything* out, and then each person can put the stuff they want on their own split.

**You need: three or four different kinds**
**of ice cream**
**marshmallow fluff**
**nuts, or nuts in syrup**
**maraschino cherries**
**canned peaches**
**frozen (but thawed)**
**raspberries, peaches,**

128

strawberries or any other
fruit
chocolate, butterscotch, or
any flavor syrup you like
bananas
whipped cream
currant, apple jelly, or any
other kind of jam you like
sprinkles, chocolate chips,
shredded coconut

Assuming you can convince anyone that some family occasion (good report card? birthday? new baby in the family? first day of spring? raise? shopping spree?) is important enough to splurge this way, all you have to do then is put out all the ingredients and enough spoons, dishes, and split bananas so everybody can make their own.

# PART 3—
# Life
# In and
# Outside
# The
# Kids'
# Kitchen

# After You Have Caught A Fish

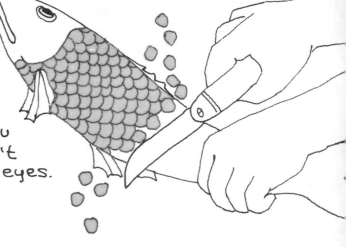

Scale a fish away from you so scales can't fly into your eyes.

Assuming you like to fish, somebody offers to take you fishing, and you catch a fish, you are now stuck with the job of cleaning it.

**You need: pocket knife**

*Gut the fish.* Find the fish's belly by feeling around with your hands. The belly is soft. Slit the belly open with the knife. Reach in with your fingers and pull out everything you can find. Rinse the cavity out with water. Rinse your hands and knife well also because the next step is scaling and slippery hands or knives lead to accidentally cut fingers.

*Scale the fish.* Scales on any fish overlap each other from head to tail. Hold the fish by its tail and scrape towards the head to loosen the scales. The fish's head should be pointing away from you. Starting at the tail end, hold your knife blade rather flat against the fish and scrape it away from your body. After the first few scales come off, the rest come easier because your blade can get under them. Keep scraping until you don't feel any rough places when you run your hand along the fish from tail to head. Rinse the fish well to get all the loose scales off its skin.

# To Bone A Cooked Fish

These pictures show how to get the flesh off a fish and leave the bones behind.

If you have a good idea of the pattern of a fish's bones, it is not hard to get nearly boneless meat to eat.

**You need: knife and fork, or spoon
scaled, cleaned, cooked fish**

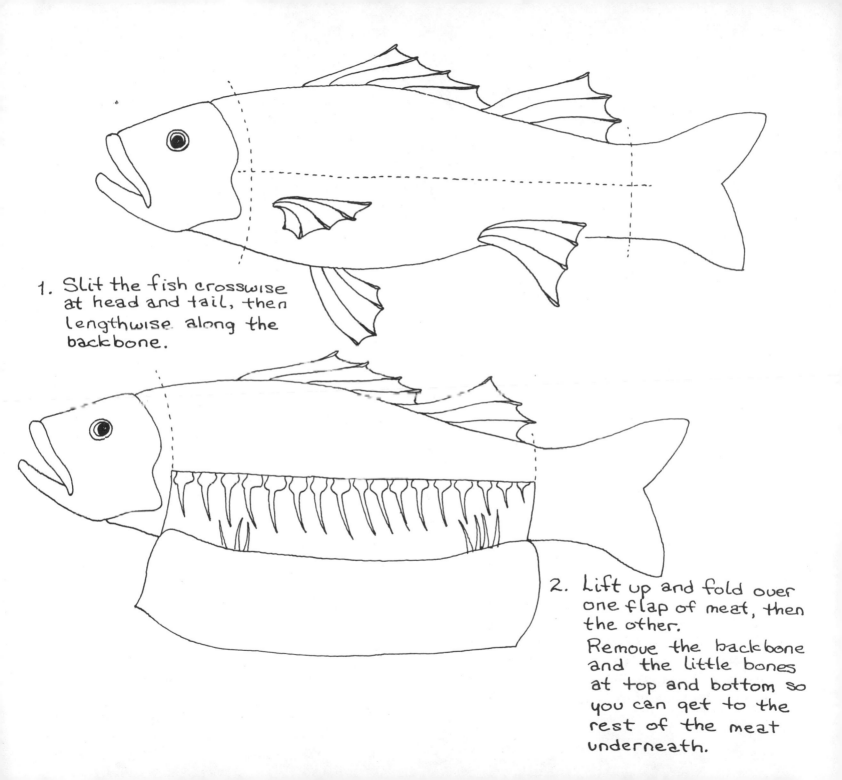

1. Slit the fish crosswise at head and tail, then lengthwise along the backbone.

2. Lift up and fold over one flap of meat, then the other.
Remove the backbone and the little bones at top and bottom so you can get to the rest of the meat underneath.

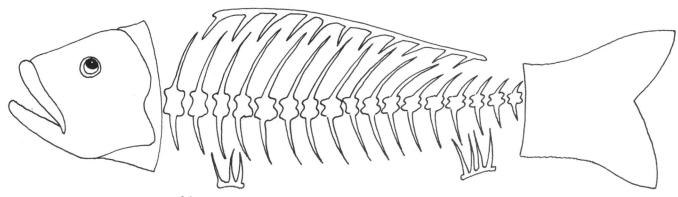

3. This is all that is left of the fish after you have eaten the boneless flesh.

Slit the fish down one side right along the center line. You'll feel the tip of your knife touching the backbone. If it still has its head and tail on, also make slits just short of the tail and gills.

Lift both flaps of meat up and over so the skin is down on the plate and the flesh turned up. The meat usually stays in one piece. If you've done it gently, all the ribs should still be in place and attached to the backbone.

The only other bones to worry about are the ones in little strips along the top and bottom edge of the fish. Fiddle with your knife until you see these strips easily, then just cut through the skin of the meat next to the bones, leaving them behind.

Lift the backbone off and throw it away. It should come off in one piece. Throw out the head and tail too, unless somebody wants to nibble on them. Detach the small strips of bone and any stray bones that might have been left behind from the remaining piece of meat.

This method should give everybody almost boneless fish — but chew carefully anyhow.

# The Missing Cod Bone

There is was. The unique, never-before-heard-of-crafts project for *The Kids' Kitchen Takeover:* A tiny perfect fish pendant made

134

from a slim, streamlined bone. We inquired at the crafts shop as to the method. Perfectly easy, we were told. Get the head of a cod fish. Boil it. Take it apart. Find the cheek bone. Paint it to look like a fish. Varnish it, and ta da! A gleaming miniature fish, caught in mid-swim with his body curved as only a fish can curve.

As luck would have it, the local fish house had a plethora of cod heads. They were huge. We took three. As we unwrapped the heads in the kitchen at home, we realized too late that they were at least yesterday's cod. Maybe last week's. They stunk. But never mind. Game for anything, we threw the heads in a pot and set them to boil. They kept right on stinking.

After an hour or so, the heads had stopped staring at us with glazed and bulky eyes. In fact, they had dissolved into a sort of gel. We took the pot down by the waterfront, let it cool down, and set to work. With our hands. Each hunk of goo, each jellied eye and

viscous gill we pored over, nose in air, with frantic fingers. Where exactly is a cod's cheek? We pulled out every sort of head bone, gill bone, eye bone, skull bone, neck bone, nose bone. Do cods *have* cheeks? Of the six pretty little fish shaped bones that were supposed to reside in those repulsive heads, we didn't find a one. You will notice that the finished product is missing from this book.

But what I want to know is, was somebody putting us on?

# Sea Urchins

Most sea urchins you find are dead, their insides already eaten by gulls. This is a shame because sea urchin roe (eggs) is terrific to eat. If you find a live sea urchin, in waters that are not polluted, break open the bottom with a pocket knife and look inside. If you see pinkish or coral-colored stuff shaped like a star, that's the roe. Scoop it out and eat it raw, or you can steam it in a tiny bit of water or butter. It's not fishy, peculiar or disgusting — just mild and lovely.

If you want to hunt for sea urchins, the time to do it is at night or very, very early morning at low tide. The urchins stay in very deep water during daylight hours but climb during the night, when you can find them under the water with a flashlight in rocky areas.

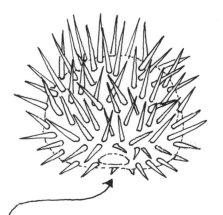

The sea urchin's roe is inside his shell. Break open the bottom with a pocket knife to find it.

# Jonah Crabs

There are some kinds of crabs that aren't sold in markets because the meat is only in the two large claws and hard to get out. In Maine, there is a crab that bothers the lobstermen because it gets into the lobster traps all the time. It is called a Jonah crab and you can get them free or·next to free.

**You need: crabs**
            **lobster fork or pick**
            **mayonnaise**

Only live crabs are safe to cook. The cooking will kill them. Boil the crabs until they turn red. Throw away the bodies and save the claws. Pick out the meat with a lobster fork, or pick and eat cold with mayonnaise. There is no sense trying to eat these crabs hot with melted butter. By the time you get the meat out of the claws, they won't be hot anymore.

If you are not in New England, ask about crabs where you live anyway. There might be another kind of local crab or fresh water crayfish that no one bothers with, that would make a very long and good meal.

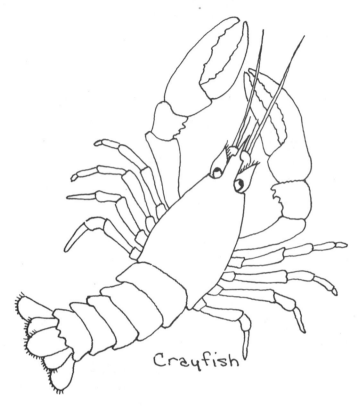

Crayfish

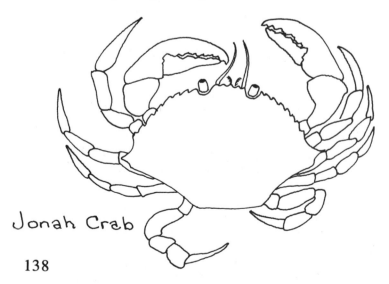

Jonah Crab

# Clamming

Half the fun of eating clams is digging them. Soft-shelled clams, or steamers, live under the mud or sand of salt water flats. People go clamming at low tide, when they can walk out onto the flats. You can tell if clams are living in the flats if you see their air holes — groups of tiny pits, that sometimes squirt water if you step near them. Before you decide to eat a clam, *check that the area isn't polluted!* Any local authority — coast guard, state police, or game warden — will know which areas have clams that are safe to eat.

**You need: old clothes**
**garden fork**
**box to put clams into**

If you are lucky, the flats will be sandy, not too hard to walk on and not too hard to dig in. If you are unlucky, they will be deep gushy mud and you may decide right away not to bother. Or they may be rocky, and you will decide after five minutes not to bother. In any case, wear your worst clothes and a pair of old sneakers so that you don't hurt your feet. Take along a garden fork and something to put the clams into. Real clammers have a wooden box called a hod made from slats and a special rake with long, slightly curved tines and a short handle. You don't need either.

When you find a group of squirt holes, start to gently dig a hole. A clam has a soft shell and if you dig hard and fast you might put the tines of the fork right through and kill it. Work with your hands too, scooping the sand out of the hole. When you see a clam, get it quickly because it can squirm deeper into the sand rather fast.

Keep "farming" the hole by digging it deeper and wider. A finished hole is about a foot deep and maybe a couple of feet wide. If you don't find more than one or two clams in the first few minutes, look for another likely place to start a new hole.

If the clamming area is good, you should be able to get enough clams to feed your family in an hour. Please don't take any clams that are less than two inches long — they are babies and should be allowed to grow up and have babies of their own.

Steamer clam (with "neck") and mussel (with "beard").

**Steaming — And Eating — Clams**
Clams should be eaten the same day you dig them. Sort through them and throw out any that are open or broken, since these might be dead clams that could make you sick.

139

**You need: clams**
**butter**
**mussels (if you find any)**
**lemon juice, chopped**
**parsley, garlic (optional)**

Wash the clams in cold water. If you let them soak in a sinkful of water for a while, they will be more likely to squirt out any sand they have inside them. Pour an inch or so of water in a big pot. Put the clams in. Get the pot boiling.

Meanwhile melt some butter. When the clams open, they are done. To eat, pull each clam out of its shell by its long "neck," dip it into melted butter, give the neck a squeeze as you slip it into your mouth and pull off the outside skin, which you then throw away.

If, when you clam, you also see some bunches of mussels, pull the larger ones from the bunch and take them home with you. They can be cooked in exactly the same way. Wash them well and pull off the stringy "beards" that hang from one edge of the shell. If you want to get fancy, flavor the melted butter with some lemon juice, chopped parsley, or garlic.

# Grow A Sunflower

If you have a place for it, a sunflower is a

fine thing to grow. You can start it in the kitchen, but then you'll have to transplant it outdoors. Vacant lots make fine gardens, and probably no one would mind that the land is not yours.

### You need: sunflower seeds
### peat pot

Stores sell the seeds in packets or you can find the seeds in a birdseed mixture — they are the large oval-shaped ones. Follow the instructions for planting and tending on the sunflower seed packet or plant an inch deep in peat pots and put the pots in the ground outdoors by late May. Once the plants start growing you will see that the name is no exaggeration — these giant flowers not only look like the sun, but move their faces to follow it all day long.

The new seeds form in the center of the flower. In the fall, when the new seeds are ripe, you can use them to feed birds, eat them raw yourself — they are extraordinarily high in protein and taste sweet — or you can save them in the freezer and plant them next spring.

# Gourds

Making things out of gourds is not much work, but it does take a long time since the gourds dry very slowly. You can grow your own or buy them at most markets and roadside stands in the fall.

Even if you have only a back yard, a corner of a vacant lot, or a big window box on a balcony, gourds are easy to grow. The seeds are cheap, the plants don't need much care, and they grow like Jack's beanstalk. Get a seed package with more than one variety, because then you won't know quite what to expect and will be surprised to see what the gourds turn out to be.

Follow the directions on the package. The gourds will form from the base of the flowers, and you might be able to guess from their tiny shapes what they will look like when they're ripe. Resist the temptation to pick them too soon. If you pick them while the skins are still thin and soft enough to cut through with your fingernail they'll soon rot and you won't be able to use them for anything. When the skin feels like a shell and you can only dent it with your fingernail if you press really hard, pick or buy the gourd. At this point, just use the gourds for decoration in a bowl or basket on a table.

After you have used the gourds for two weeks as decoration, find a warm dry place to spread them out to dry. It takes quite a long time — sometimes weeks, sometimes months, and only some of the gourds will dry. If any begin to rot, throw them out right away

143

Some common
gourd shapes,
including ones that look
just like eggs.

You can paint
a face on your
roly poly and
add yarn for
hair.

This rattle
handle is still too
big to fit the hole.
Whittle it little
by little.

Beans make a different
sound than rice.

Covering egg-shaped
gourds with papier
mâché makes them
easier to decorate.
Use small pieces of
paper

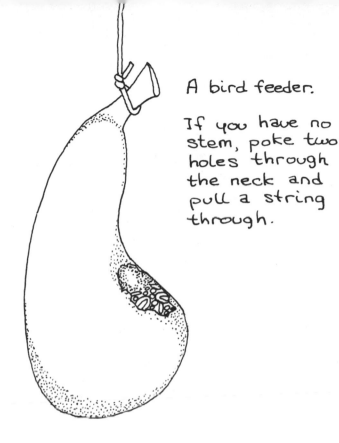

A bird feeder.

If you have no stem, poke two holes through the neck and pull a string through.

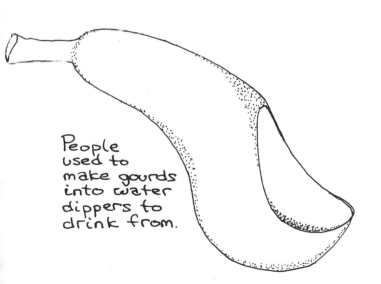

People used to make gourds into water dippers to drink from.

to keep the other ones safe. As the gourds dry, they fade. Sometimes they even turn a tan color. They will feel lighter when you pick them up. Parts of the shell will be hard enough to make a clicking noise when you tap them lightly with your fingernail. After an even longer time, they will feel very light and if you shake one, the seeds inside will rattle. The gourd is now ready to make into something interesting. Here are a few ideas.

**Roly Poly**

If you have a pear-shaped gourd with a round bottom, you can make a roly poly — one of those dolls that you push down only to see it roll right up again.

**You need: pear-shaped gourd**
**sharp knife**
**nuts, bolts, lead curtain**
**weights, or any other small**
**heavy objects**
**liquid white glue**
**paint (acrylic works best)**

Cut the top of the gourd off with a very sharp, pointed knife. Do it as neatly as you can, because you are going to glue it back on again later. Dump out the dry shreds and seeds that are inside. Find some nuts, bolts, lead curtain weights or any other small heavy things. Glue them into a pile at the very

145

bottom of the gourd. You may have to let a layer of them dry before you try to glue on more. When you think you have a good heavy mound down there, test out the roly poly by pushing it down and see if it bounces back up again. If it doesn't, add more small weights, or try a rounder gourd. When it works, glue the top back on. Then paint it any way you want. A roly poly makes a good present.

## Maraca

Since the seeds in a dry gourd already rattle, it isn't hard to make the gourd into a maraca.

**You need: gourd**
**sharp knife**
**stick**
**liquid white glue**
**paint (acrylic works best)**

Cut the stem out of the gourd with a sharp knife. This should make a hole that's not too big. Then find a stick that fits into the hole tightly — one slightly bigger than the hole is best, because then you can whittle it to size. Cut it as long as you want the handle to be. Glue it in place, and paint and varnish the maraca if you like it fancy.

## Bird Feeder

**You need: gourd**

**string**
**knife**
**awl**

Cut a hole with a sharp knife somewhere in the side of the gourd. This is so small birds can perch on its edge and you will have a place to pour the birdseed into. Make two more small holes on the top with an awl so you can push a string through to hang the feeder up. If the stem on the gourd is large enough, of course, you could tie the string to that.

## Christmas Gourds

Because gourds lose most of their color after they're dry, they don't make very good decorations anymore. But their shapes are still so pretty, it's tempting to do nature one better by a little redecorating. There are two ways.

**You need: acrylic or tempera paint (you**
**might need sandpaper or**
**liquid detergent with**
**tempera)**
**gourd**
**shellac or clear varnish spray**

Paint the gourd in any pattern you like, using acrylic paints if you don't feel like shellacking or varnishing it, or tempera paints if that's what you have in the house.

If the tempera paint doesn't go on easily,

there may be natural wax on the surface of the gourd. You can either sand it off with sandpaper or you can mix a few drops of liquid detergent with the tempera paint and see if that helps. When the paint is dry, shellac the gourd or spray it with varnish.

### Papier Mâché Gourds

Another way to decorate gourds is to cover them with papier mâché.

**You need: liquid white glue**
**saucer or cereal bowl**
**shredded paper (towels,**
**newspaper, or brown**
**paper)**
**gourd**
**paint**
**shellac or clear varnish spray**

Thin white glue with a little water in a saucer or a cereal bowl. Tear paper into small shreds — you can use paper towels, newspaper, or brown paper. Newspaper's probably the easiest. Dip a shred of paper in the glue, and smooth it over the gourd. Keep doing that until the gourd is covered with two layers or so. If you want a really smooth finish, do the last layer with bits of paper towel, because the torn edges are thin and don't show much. Let the papier mâché dry overnight, then paint and varnish the gourd.

# Terraria

A terrarium is any glass container planted with small plants that will grow under moist and shady conditions. The glass container acts as a greenhouse, keeping the plants moist and warm.

**You need: container**
**charcoal**
**pebbles**
**soil**
**plants**
**plastic bags**
**gardening trowel or kitchen**
**spoon**

*Choose a container.* A fishbowl with a narrow neck works very well. Large mayonnaise jars are fine too, as long as you can get your hand down to the bottom without too much trouble. A lid will keep the air and soil damp longer without watering, but is not usually necessary.

*Prepare the jar.* The floor of a terrarium is made up of three layers. First put down a layer of broken up charcoal. Charcoal will keep things in the terrarium from rotting. A burnt-up log from the fireplace will do, or

charcoal briquettes if you can break them. Next comes a layer of pebbles. The pebbles are simply to make sure water drains away from the roots of the plants. You can use driveway gravel, or the gravel they sell in pet stores. Next comes the soil. Use soil from the place where you gather the plants, because then you'll be sure it's the right soil for the plants you choose. You should have two inches of soil.

*Collect the plants.* Plants that do well under the same conditions tend to grow near one another. A terrarium is a moist environment much like woodland, so the place to look for plants that will grow well together in a moist container is in the woods. Bring plastic bags and a gardening trowel or kitchen spoon with you. Walk along until you come to a spot where a variety of small plants and mosses are growing. Old favorites that do well are: partridge berry, miniature ferns, rattlesnake plantain, false lily of the valley, myrtle, ground pine, and wintergreen (a flavoring for chewing gum — chew on a leaf and see).

If you see a lovely little plant, check around first to make sure it isn't a young plant that will grow much bigger. If it is small because it is still growing, it will outgrow your terrarium too soon. Tiny trees will attract you. Resist. They don't transplant well from the woods and will die.

149

Before you dig up any plants, gather enough soil in one of the bags for the floor of your terrarium. Also look around for a small moss-covered stone, or a rotting bit of bark or twig with interesting lichens or fungus growing on it. Collect mosses of several kinds. Dig up the plants last of all so they will not be out of the ground for too long. Dig down as deep and as gently as you can. Lift the plant out carefully, and put it right into its own plastic bag.

If you are digging plants like partridge berry or ground pine, which are vine-like and have roots along the strands, pull gently on fronds and strands to find the center of the plant where the most mature roots will be. (In some states, it is against the conservation laws to pick ground pine, because people have depleted it by clearing woodlands for houses and by gathering it for Christmas wreaths. Check first.)

If you can't find woodland plants growing

From left to right, these terrarium plants are false lily of the valley, wintergreen, miniature fern, rattlesnake plantain, ground pine and partridgeberry.

naturally where you live — or if you aren't allowed to dig them up — dime stores sell various miniature plants that do well in terraria. Ask for plants that stay tiny and appreciate moisture.

*Assembling the terrarium.* When you get your plants home, put the soil into the jar or bowl and plant your plants right away. Water them and press them firmly into the soil. Then you can place your pieces of moss over the soil to make a lovely green carpet, and put a mossy stone or lichen-covered twig where it looks nice. Use a bit of crumpled paper towel to clean the dirt off the inside of the glass.

A terrarium with woodland plants doesn't need direct sun. Any bright spot suits it. You should only have to water it about once a week, because the shape of the terrarium cuts down evaporation. The best way to water it is with a spray bottle. There's no need to buy one: Bottles like Windex sprayers work just as well. If your house or apartment is very dry, a piece of cardboard over the top of your terrarium will keep it moist enough.

# Dried Flowers

Some flowers, grasses and seed pods need no special treatment to dry. You can just hang them upside down in small loose bunches in any place that is airy and dry. The sun will bleach them, so keep them under a roof, on a porch, in a well-ventilated attic, shed or barn. We had no trouble drying flowers by hanging them from our livingroom wall.

Some of the common dried flowers, grasses and pods you find in stores may grow near your home and are worth trying to dry yourself. They are strawflowers, tansy, sumac, mullein, cattail, teasel, millet, ailanthus, mimosa, black locust, honesty, rose of Sharon, poppy, gas plant.

Strawflowers can be bought in seed packets if you can't find them growing wild. They come in several colors and varieties.

Many flowers that don't dry well naturally can be dried by another method.

**You need: zinnia, marigold or chrysanthemum flowers**
**commercial silicon gel (Flower-Dri®) or very fine sand (collect it by sifting sea sand through a strainer)**
**shoebox or similar container**
**thin florist's wire**
**can, jar, or vase**

Start with a sturdy flower like a zinnia, marigold or chrysanthemum. Pick the flowers when they are still young so you don't work

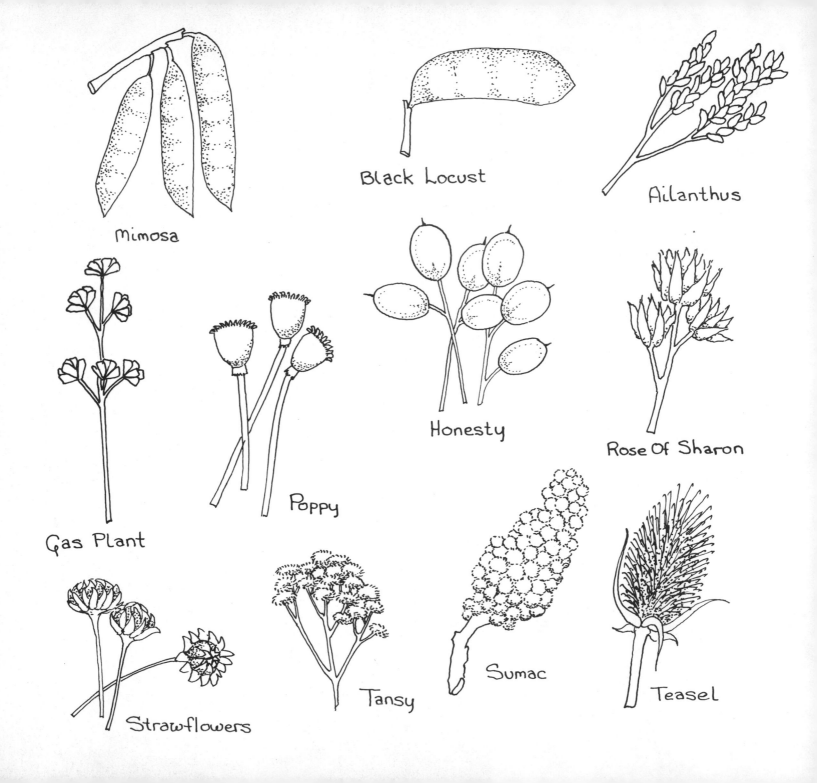

Mimosa

Black Locust

Ailanthus

Gas Plant

Poppy

Honesty

Rose Of Sharon

Strawflowers

Tansy

Sumac

Teasel

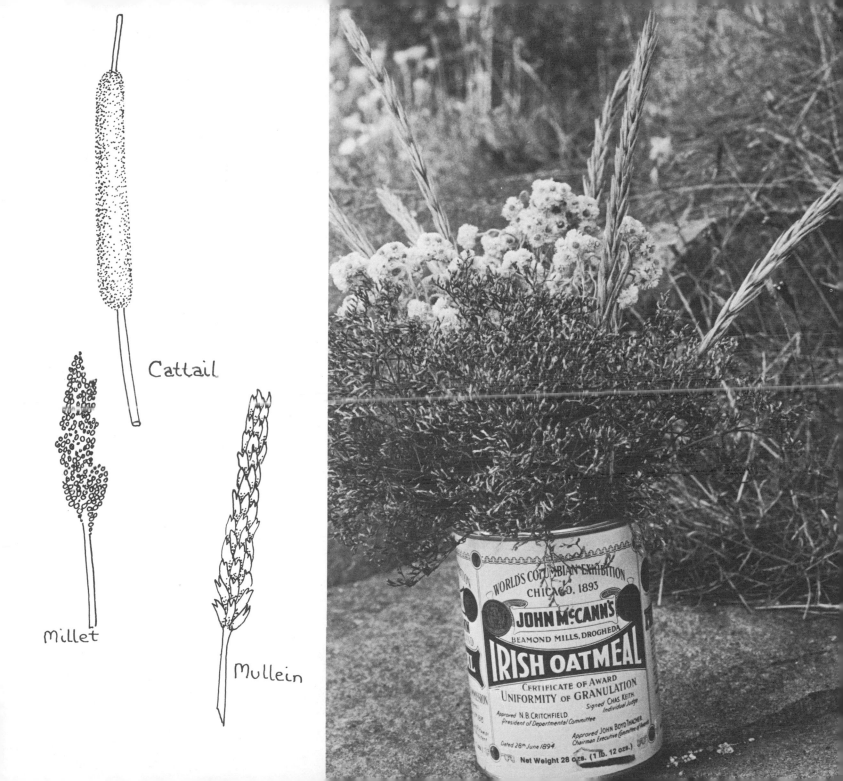

Cattail

Millet

Mullein

with one that is about to fall apart. Leave an inch or so of stem on the flower. Pour an inch of gel or sand into the container and stick the stems of the flowers into it. Leave plenty of

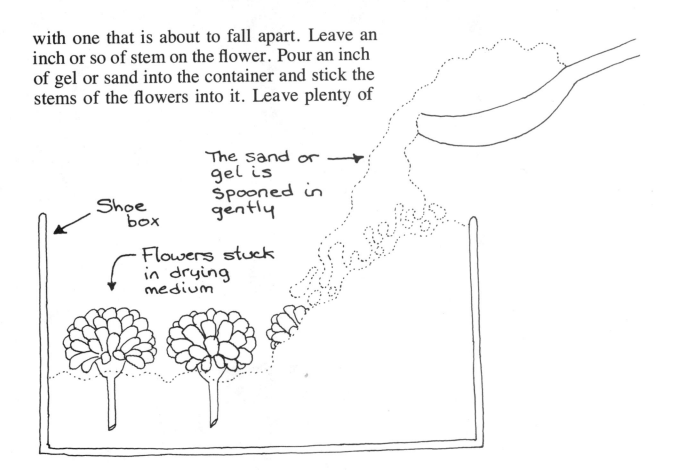

The sand or gel is spooned in gently

Shoe box

Flowers stuck in drying medium

room around each flower. Gently pour in more of the gel or sand until the blossoms are completely covered. Cover the container and go away. If you are using sand, you should not even peek for a week or more. The gel works faster. Directions on the package will tell you what to expect.

When the flowers are dry, pour the gel or sand off gently. You'll probably have to brush some of it off the flowers also. Use an artist's brush. To make a flower arrangement, twist florist's wire around each small piece of stem and arrange the flowers in a can, jar, or vase.

# Potpourri

Sometimes things smell so good in the

summer or fall that you wish you could keep the smells to sniff through the winter. You can't keep all the good smells — like fresh cut grass or burning leaves — but there are many you can trap in bottles or jars to sniff whenever you like. Mixtures of leaves and flowers that are dried and kept for their perfume are called "potpourri," which literally means, I'm afraid, "pot of rotten stuff."

**You need: leaves, needles, blossoms or berries of plants like bayberry, juniper, pine, roses (wild roses are best), lavender, aromatic lemon or rose geraniums (these are not pretty but the plants smell wonderful and are inexpensive), mint, sage, thyme, rosemary, or other herbs**
**cookie sheet or cardboard dress-box tops**
**jars with lids**
**lemon or orange peels**
**vegetable peeler**
**cloves, mace, cinnamon**

Spread the leaves, needles or petals on a cookie sheet, the top of a dress box, or even a sheet of cardboard. They should be spread thin enough so nothing is piled on top of

anything else. Dry them out of the sun if you want to keep their color — sunlight bleaches. When they are very dry, and when the day is a dry one too, mix the ingredients whose smells seem to go together. Smells go together when they smell good to you. Put the potpourri in jars and screw the tops on tight.

If the plants that grow near you don't smell good, you can peel lemon and oranges very thinly with a vegetable peeler, dry them, and cheat a little by adding a couple of cloves or some mace or cinnamon. It isn't as adventurous but it smells just as good.

# Crystallized Rose Petals

Crystallized flowers are a fuss to make but good to eat.

**You need: rose petals (wild roses taste best)**
**1 raw egg white**
**waxed paper**
**granulated sugar**

Don't gather the rose petals until you feel like crystallizing them. Otherwise they wilt and are unusable.

Beat the egg white to make it a little foamy. Dip your fingers in the foam, smear it around both sides of a petal, and put it down on waxed paper. You'll get tired after the first couple of dozen but that's enough anyway. Place each petal far away from the others so they don't stick to one another. Before they dry, wash the egg white off your hands and sprinkle granulated sugar on the petals. Turn them over and do the other side.

Put them in a warm place that's out of the sun to dry. It should only take a day or so for them to dry enough to eat. They do taste good.

# Wild Foods To Try

### Berries
When people actually lived on nuts, berries, and roots that they collected, collecting probably was a full-time business. Wild foods are small and hard to find. A day of gathering feeds a family of six, if all six gather, and if all six refrain from nibbling as they go. Nevertheless, curiosity has moved us to try Nature's miniature bounty from time to time.

Fruits and berries are the best for beginners: there are more of them, one knows in advance how they taste, and some of them can just be

popped in the mouth raw. One warning: don't eat anything unless you are sure what it is you are eating and that it is edible. The fruits and berries mentioned here are either common enough so that almost everyone recognizes them, or they are illustrated so you can identify them.

You can eat these fruits as you go: raspberries, blueberries, blackberries, wild strawberries, and concord grapes (they make good jelly too).

These fruits make delicious sauces, jams or jellys: crabapples, gooseberries, quinces, currants, elderberries, rose hips, beach plums, barberries, cranberries, and sour cherries (small red cherries that are better used in a pie).

## Cattails

Wild foods like cattails are for the more adventurous. Cut the stalks at or a little below the ground. The stalk ends in a white part like

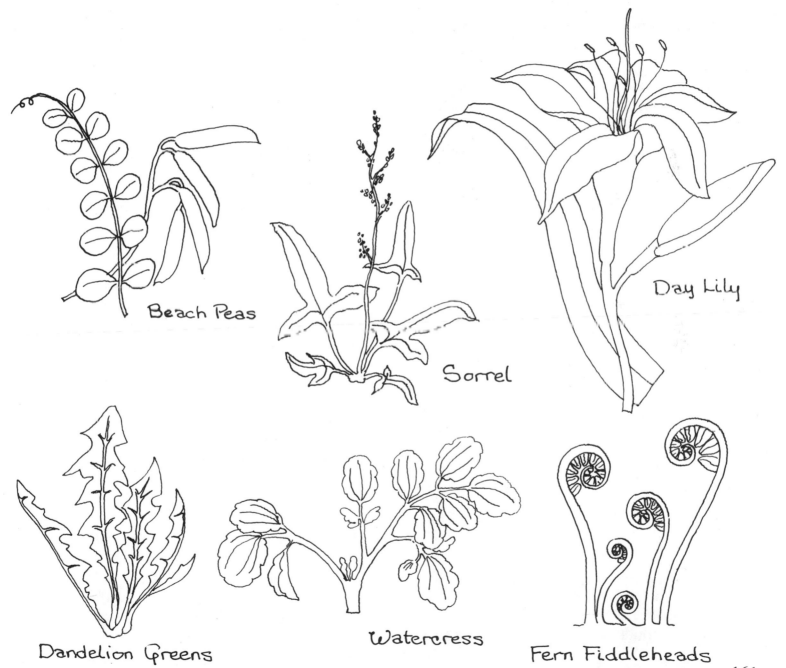

Beach Peas

Sorrel

Day Lily

Dandelion Greens

Watercress

Fern Fiddleheads

the tender bottom of a stalk of grass. Peel off one or two layers of the greener outside leaves just as you would peel a scallion. Again like a scallion, cut off the white end (about six or eight inches on a cattail). Then split the white part lengthwise, and cook it in some butter over a low heat. It tastes vaguely "green" and cucumberish.

### Beach Peas

If you live near the Atlantic ocean, you will probably find beach peas. They look and taste like regular peas and can be boiled the same way, but they are tiny and starchier.

### Fiddleheads

The tender "fiddleheads" of ferns — the curled sprout that comes up in early spring — can be boiled with a little water and eaten as a vegetable. A couple of minute's cooking is enough. The fiddleheads are also good raw in salads, as are several common weeds like sheep sorrel, dandelion leaves (cut just after they sprout in spring or they will be very bitter), and wild watercress.

### Day Lilies

These green plants grow in clumps and blossom with pale orange flowers along roadsides in July. They can be eaten from top to bottom — buds, roots, tubers, and leaves.

The green buds are good boiled for only a few minutes — rescue them from the pot before they get too soft — and then served with melted butter. Both the buds and the withered blossoms can be added to soups and stews. If you dig under the lily plant, you will find small white tubers clinging to the roots. Choose crisp young ones. Cut off the bits of root sticking out and either eat them raw (plain or in salad), or boil them briefly so they are crisp not soft, drain them, and add butter. Don't worry about hurting the lily plants. They appreciate thinning, and grow all the more vigorously.

You can also eat the sprouts of the day lily in early spring, before they become tough. Snip them off at ground level, throw away the outside leaves, and put the tender inside leaves in a salad or cook them just like cattails.

# Tap A Maple Tree

If you have sugar maples in your backyard or nearby, try tapping it and turning the sap into maple sugar.

The sap of sugar maples begins to rise in about the middle of February, and runs for about a month and a half.

**You need: brace and bit**
             **drill**
             **hammer**
             **tap***
             **nail (optional)**
             **bucket with a handle**
             **very large pot with a lid**
             **cheesecloth and strainer**
             **sterilized bottle or jar**

Choose a bit the same size as the tap, and drill a straight hole two inches into the tree at a convenient height. Hammer the tap into the hole.

Hang the bucket from the tap or from a nail above it. The sap will flow through the tap into the bucket. Empty the sap into the big pot every day. The flow depends on the weather

*You will have to buy the tap. It costs very little and is available from the New Canaan Nature Center, New Canaan, Connecticut 06840.*

Leaf of a sugar maple

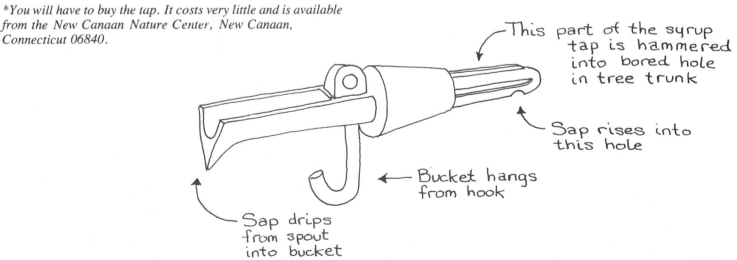

This part of the syrup tap is hammered into bored hole in tree trunk

Sap rises into this hole

Bucket hangs from hook

Sap drips from spout into bucket

but an average tree will yield approximately twenty gallons per season. Cover the pot and keep it in the refrigerator.

Boil the sap down on a low flame, which takes forever. (As much as two full days for a large soup pot of sap.) Forty gallons of sap boils down to only one gallon of syrup, ten gallons boils down to a quart, five gallons to a pint. Even very big soup pots hold only about five gallons, but a whole pint of maple syrup is not to be sneered at.

When the sap has become a syrup, as thick as heavy cream and golden in color, strain it through cheesecloth in a strainer to get out bits of stuff, and pour it into a sterilized bottle. If the bottle isn't sterilized, refrigerate the syrup and use it within the next few weeks.

# Burr Furniture

Big burdock weeds grow just about everywhere in America. Try to locate a couple of good plants before the burdocks come into bloom in late August.

Pick the burrs and use them to make miniature furniture while they are still green. Burrs have prickles and stay together easily. Each prickle ends in a tiny hook, and these hooks cling to one another like hands

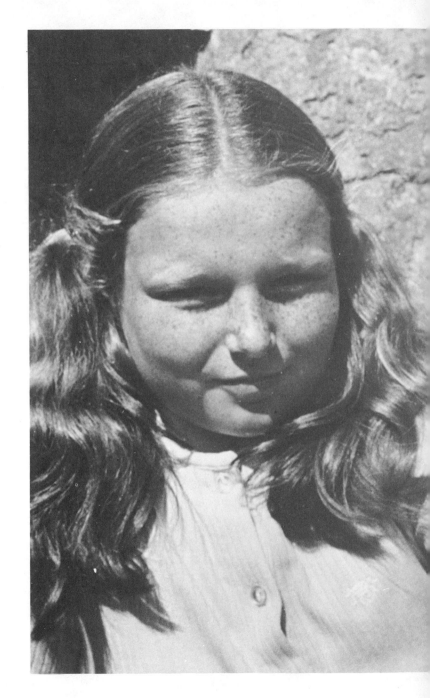

clasping. Put them on the refrigerator or windowsill to dry. Burr beds, chairs, couches, or tables will stay strong and playable all winter.

# Cake Pan Gardens

Cake pan gardens don't last forever, but they look like a little world of their own while they do. All you need is a cake pan, and any rocks, moss, lichens, twigs, or grass tufts you see and like. Even city parks may offer bits of moss or little weeds that no one would mind you taking.

**You need:** **soil**
**cake pan**
**moss**
**rocks**
**plants**
**spray bottle**

Fill the bottom of the pan with about one inch of soil. Arrange the moss and rocks on the soil first. The more kinds of moss you use, the more interesting the garden will look. Tree seedlings won't survive in such shallow soil, but dry twigs can make a little winter

forest, or a craggy branch could look like an ancient tree. Experiment with a few other sorts of plants. The cake pan garden in the photograph lasted for a summer, watered every day with a spray bottle, and it didn't need direct sun.

# Sponge Grass

Just for fun, especially if you are tired of winter and would like to see a little patch of grass, try growing a lawn on a sponge.

**You need: clean sponge**
**dish**
**grass seed**

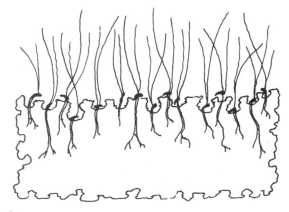

Grass roots grow down through the holes of the sponge.

Put a clean, wet sponge on a dish and sprinkle grass seed over it. Keep the sponge moist by dribbling water on it every day. The seeds will sprout in about a week, and the grass roots will grow down into the moist sponge. Eventually lack of nourishment will kill the lawn, but it only takes a week to start a new one.

If it amuses you, cut the sponge into the shape of an animal first. Of course, if you'd rather, there's nothing wrong with growing the grass in a regular flower pot. Or try clover!

# The Great Avocado

Of all the pits, seeds, roots, and tubers that grow in a kitchen, the avocado is king. People love their avocado plants. They talk to them. They feel each has its own personality. An avocado tree becomes part of the family.

**You need:** **avocado pit**
**3 toothpicks or skewers**
**glass, cup, or custard dish**
**flower pot**
**soil**

Cut open an avocado and take out the pit.

Sometimes the pit looks closed up tight, as though it would never sprout. Sometimes it has already cracked, and the root is beginning to push out the bottom. Tightly shut pits may not sprout for many weeks; occasionally, one won't sprout at all. If you want to be certain the pit will grow, wait until you find a pit that has started to sprout by itself.

Stick three toothpicks or skewers into the pit near the top (narrow) end of the pit. Place the avocado in a glass, cup, or custard dish so that the toothpicks rest on the rim and the thick end is in the water. Keep the glass filled with water. If you keep it near the kitchen sink you'll have a better chance of remembering to stick it under the faucet and refill it to the top every day. The roots will grow for quite a while before the top begins to sprout. The plant grows very slowly. When you have nursed your baby tree to the point where you have a sprout with several sets of leaves on it, some people advise snipping off the top pair to encourage the plant to put out side branches. Other people say not to bother. If your pit was the small smooth type, it won't branch much no matter what you do; if it was the large crinkly type, it will branch whether you pinch it or not. When the roots look strong, or when the top has begun to sprout, you can plant your pit in a pot of soil with about a third of the pit sticking up from the dirt. Keep the plant in a sunny place and water it often as it grows into a tree.

# Mold Gardens

Molds like yeasts, live in the air, and need only a nice place to grow to become visible to you. They are plants. Different molds prefer different things to grow on. To get a garden that has blue molds, green molds, black molds, possibly even the rarer pink and orange molds, you have to offer them a variety of foods.

**You need: pie plate**
**bread and jelly, rice, orange**
**peel, cheddar cheese**
**aluminum foil**
**magnifying glass (optional)**

Get a large pie plate. Arrange on it a piece of bread, a few dabs of different kinds of jelly or jam, some orange peel, a little rice and some cheddar cheese. Watch out for foods with preservatives, because the preservatives were meant to kill molds. Sprinkle a little water over everything. Cover the plate loosely with a piece of aluminum foil — not airtight, just to keep the water from evaporating too fast. Put the plate in a cupboard or closet

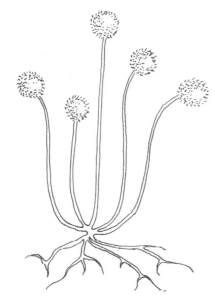

This is an ordinary bread mold, magnified many times.

where it will stay dark. Check and water it often enough to keep the foods moist.

When molds begin to grow, they're interesting to look at through a magnifying glass.

# Windowsill Herb Garden

An herb garden is probably one of the easiest and most pleasurable gardens to grow, even if you have only an indoor windowsill to grow it on. You can grow herbs winter or summer. Your kitchen will smell good all the time, and the fresh herbs taste much better in cooking than dry ones. There is one limitation: You can't plant the herbs that grow very large, like lavender. But then you don't need lavender to cook with anyhow.

**You need:** **clay pots**
**soil**
**sand**
**herb plants or seeds**
**spray bottle**
**scissors**
**string**

Herbs do best in clay pots filled with good garden soil (you can buy it if you don't have any outside) mixed with coarse sand. Use one measure of sand for every two measures of soil. If you can't get sand easily, pet stores carry coarse sand for aquariums. The herb plants usually need to be watered only once a week, but sometimes in the winter the air gets so dry that they should be misted from a spray bottle a few times a week too. All herbs need sun.

The following perennial herbs live for lots of years. You have to buy them as plants because they're hard to grow from seed. Where we live, they cost about seventy-five cents each. Chives, sage (try to get dwarf

# PERENNIAL

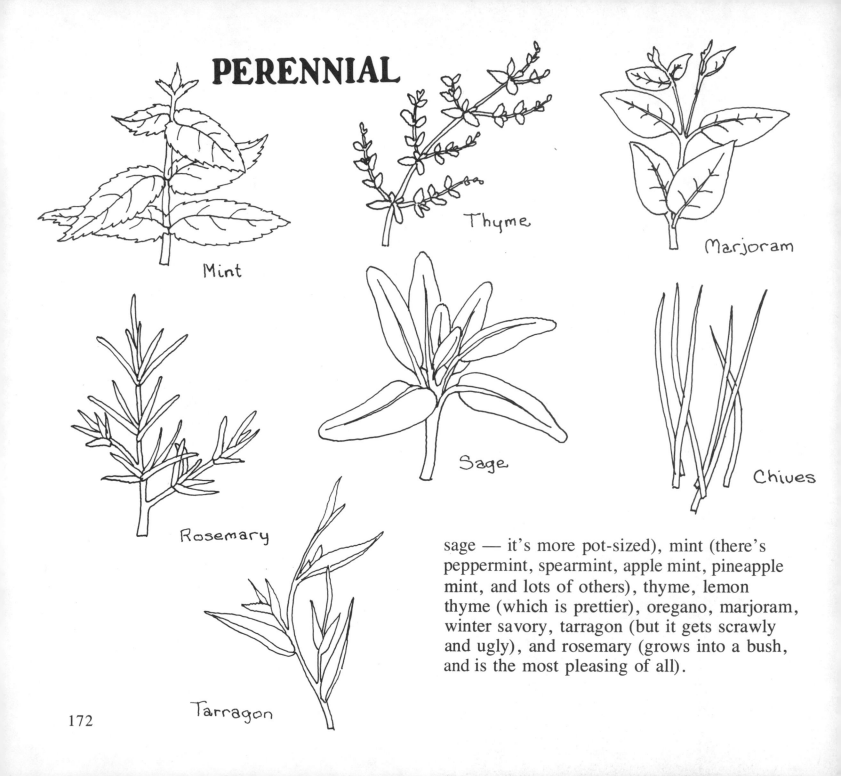

Mint

Thyme

Marjoram

Rosemary

Sage

Chives

Tarragon

sage — it's more pot-sized), mint (there's peppermint, spearmint, apple mint, pineapple mint, and lots of others), thyme, lemon thyme (which is prettier), oregano, marjoram, winter savory, tarragon (but it gets scrawly and ugly), and rosemary (grows into a bush, and is the most pleasing of all).

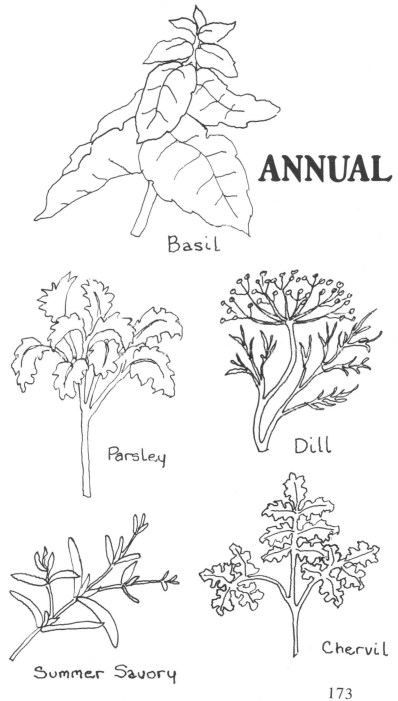

**ANNUAL**

Basil

Parsley

Dill

Summer Savory

Chervil

173

These annual herbs live for only one season and you can grow them from seed: basil, parsley, chervil, dill, and summer savory.

If you are really lucky, you may happen upon a nursery that sells sweet bay. That's where bay leaves come from. The plant is apparently hard to get started and is quite expensive. But once you have one, you'll have all the bay leaves you can ever use from a great-looking bush that's green and easy to care for winter and summer.

About the only fault herbs have is that they get scraggly looking. If you keep snipping them back, though, they'll stay bushy and windowsill-sized. They can take a lot of snipping.

Once you have fresh herbs around, you'll probably want to try oregano in tuna fish sandwiches, sage leaves in lemonade, and mint on a banana split. Don't restrain yourself.

If you want to dry herbs for gifts or to add to a potpourri, snip off small bunches of them still on their stems, tie a string around them, and hang them up in the house. When the weather is too damp for them to dry, remove the bottom rack from the oven, hang the herbs from the top rack, and dry them at the lowest temperature your oven will go. You can experiment with herbal teas too. Make it the same way as ordinary tea. Mint is a good one to try.

Hang small bunches of herbs upside down to dry them

# Garbage Garden

An indoor garbage garden is an experimental agricultural station. The pits and parts of fruits and vegetables you save from the garbage may

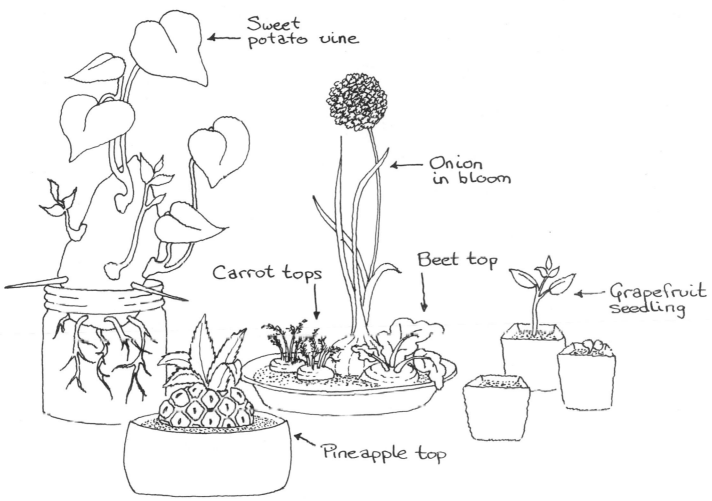

Sweet potato vine

Onion in bloom

Carrot tops

Beet top

Grapefruit seedling

Pineapple top

or may not grow into pretty plants, because the garbage gardener has no way of telling whether the seeds he or she plants are fertile or sterile, or whether tubers (like potatoes and yams) have been treated to prevent sprouting. Therefore the best attitude to take is that of the scientist who wonders, watches, and finds out.

**You need: plastic box or corrugated box lined with plastic**
**peat pots**
**soil**
**seeds, pits or pieces of vegetable**

175

The best container to use for your garden is a plastic box called a flat (they might give you one at a roadside garden store) or a corrugated box lined with a piece of plastic; fill either container with small peat pots of earth. Use bags of house-plant soil rather than dirt from outdoors. If a seed sprouts you can easily move it into a more permanent pot. If a seed doesn't sprout, plant something else in the peat container. Label each peat pot with the kind of pit it contains and the date you put it in the soil. Keep the flat or box in a sunny window. Keep the soil moist until the seeds sprout. From then on, water only when the soil gets dry. When these experimental seedlings grow to a few inches in height, you can transplant them into larger clay or plastic pots. You don't have to remove them from their peat pots — just put the peat pot into the larger new pot adding soil under and around it. The roots will grow through the peat into the new soil.

## Pits, Stones, Seeds, And Pips To Try

*Grapefruit seeds.* Plant one-half inch deep. Watch for sprouts after several weeks. They can grow into trees.

*Orange and lemon seeds.* Plant as you would grapefruit seeds. These take longer to sprout and are more sensitive plants. Don't expect too much, but they can grow into trees.

*Date pits.* Soak in water for three days. Plant one-half inch deep. They won't sprout for at least several months. Maybe they'll grow into palm trees!

*Plums, prune, peach, cherry and olive stones; apple seeds, and pear pips.* Plant one inch deep. Wait a few months for them to sprout and hope for the best. These are all trees.

*Grape seeds.* Soak in water for one week. Plant in sand or loose soil. They may take a long time to sprout, but if they grow, they will be vines. If you can get Concord grapes in the fall, they are easier to grow because they are a native wild grape.

*Pepper seeds.* Try seeds from fresh green peppers, seeds from dried chili, or cherry peppers. Sprinkle over the soil and then sprinkle a little more soil on top. They should sprout in about five to eight days.

*Pumpkin, watermelon, squash.* Try only seeds that are large and hard-shelled. Plant one-half inch deep. The pumpkin and squash seeds should sprout in four to seven days; the watermelon seeds in six to twelve days.

## Fruits And Vegetables That Sprout And Grow

*Beets, turnips, carrots, parsnips, and horseradish roots*. Choose old thick ones. Cut off the top part from which the leaves ordinarily grow and save the rest to eat. Plant the top one-quarter inch deep in loose soil or sand with the top sticking up. These will almost certainly sprout new leaves in a week or so.

*Onion*. Use an onion that has started to sprout. Plant with the sprouted top sticking up from the soil. The onion has a pretty flower which will bloom in a few months if the plant gets enough sun.

*Sweet potato*. Put in a jar of water. The end with fibers sticking out of it is the end that goes into the water. The other end should stick up out of the water. Refill with fresh water as it evaporates. After the roots grow, and leaves appear, plant it in soil. It grows very fast and turns into a terrific vine.

*Pineapple*. Cut off the top, and pull off a couple of rows of the lower leaves. Let the cut end dry for a day or two. Plant one-inch deep in soil. Keep it in the sun and moist. It won't sprout new leaves for a month or two.

# Lucky Cricket

The Chinese people have always kept crickets in little cages — crickets cheer up a house with their chirping and bring luck to the family. If you live or can spend some time outside the city you can go on a cricket hunt. They are easy to find, easy to feed and fun to listen to. This is how to find a black field cricket.

**You need: jar**
**flashlight**
**cheesecloth**
**rubber band**
**cricket food like bread in**
**milk, soft fruits, raw**
**hamburger, or cooked**
**cereal**

Wait until the beginning of August, when this year's crickets have grown up enough to chirp. Prepare a jar to catch a cricket. Bring it, and a flashlight, outside with you on the night you choose for the hunt. Stand still and listen carefully: a number of insects and frogs may be making noises. In early summer, tiny frogs might be saying "peep, peep, peep" in a high voice. Larger frogs croak "garrump, garrump." Later in the summer katydids say "katydid." But only crickets say "cheer up, cheer up." Walk towards the noise. It will stop. Now you have to stop and wait and listen. Soon the "cheer up" will start again and you can get a little closer. When you are right next to the noise, start looking with your flashlight. The cricket will very likely be under a stone or in a damp place along the foundations of a wall. Pick it up carefully since the hind legs of grasshoppers and crickets come off rather easily and put it in the jar. Take a close look to see if you've found a boy cricket, the one that makes a noise, or a non-singing girl cricket who may have been near him. The girl cricket has a long, thin

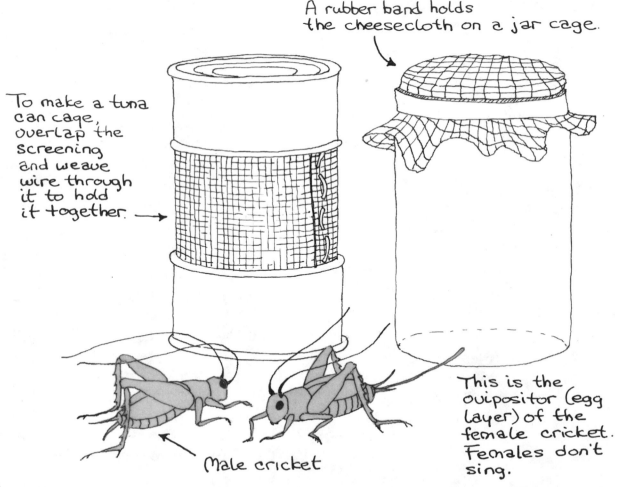

A rubber band holds the cheesecloth on a jar cage.

To make a tuna can cage, overlap the screening and weave wire through it to hold it together. →

This is the ovipositor (egg layer) of the female cricket. Females don't sing.

Male cricket

178

egg-laying device at her rear, while the boy has only two feeler-like things with nothing in the middle. If you have found a female and you'd rather have the singing male, let her go and try again.

The jar can be his permanent home if you cover the top with cheesecloth and a rubber band so enough air comes in. Or you can make a nicer home from two tuna fish cans and a piece of wire screen. Sometimes you can find a real Chinese cricket cage, with a tiny sliding door, in a gift store or mail order catalog.

Crickets are scavengers which means they eat bits of anything they find. Try bread soaked in milk, ripe banana or other soft fruits, raw hamburger, or cooked cereals. Each day, clean out the uneaten food so it doesn't spoil. You can watch your cricket eat and wash his own hands, face and antennae afterwards. You can also watch him chirp. He will crouch forward, lift his wings slightly above his back, and vibrate them against one another. At close range it's hard to believe the volume of sound he can produce. It's best to keep a cricket as a kitchen pet — he'll keep you awake if he's kept in your bedroom.

Crickets live in city parks as well as in the country. Still, if you are a city dweller, it might be safest to wait until someone invites you to the suburbs before you do any cricket hunting, rather than trying it in the park at night.

# Pet Snail

A snail is a perfect kitchen pet because it eats the outside leaves of lettuce and cabbages that you normally throw away. Of course, it doesn't eat much.

**You need: snail**
**jar**
**cheesecloth**
**rubber band**

If you find a snail (and they certainly live in damp and woody areas of city parks, not only country or suburban areas), put it in a jar with a small piece of cheesecloth secured with a rubber band as a lid. This gives the snail lots of air.

For a start, give the snail an outside leaf of lettuce to eat. Rinse out its jar and put a fresh leaf in every day. You'll be able to see the holes the snail has eaten clearly. In fact, if you watch closely, you'll see it bite its way along the edge of a leaf, or gnaw its way through the middle. Don't ever leave any pet's jar in the sun. The glass jar is like a greenhouse; it will trap enough heat to quickly kill your pet.

# Live Garbage Disposal System

If your mother can't bear to waste the outside leaves of lettuces and cabbages, and the snail isn't eating enough, and your father isn't interested in keeping a compost heap, suggest a guinea pig. A guinea pig can eat its

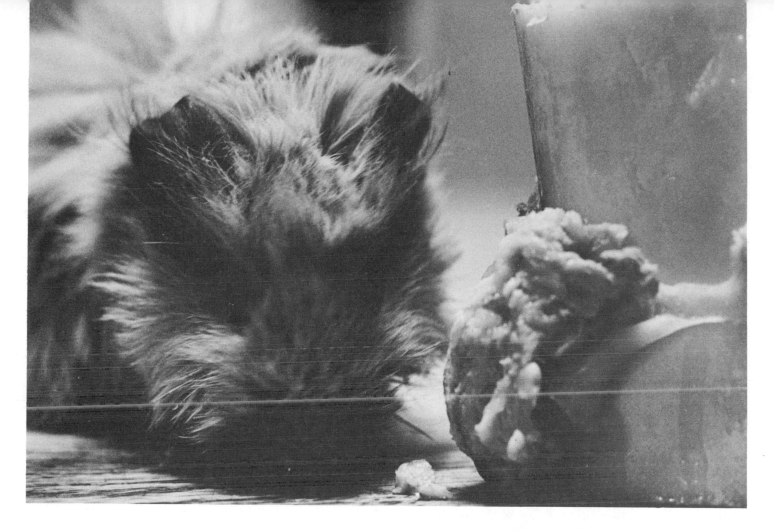

way through a day's worth of peelings and leavings like a fuzzy vacuum cleaner. It will need water too, though, and a basic diet of store-bought pellets.

**You need: guinea pig**
**small rabbit hutch or plastic**
**milk crate**
**newspaper**

Guinea pigs come in three varieties. The most common is the smooth short-haired variety. Another variety has cowlicks at the top of its head and on both sides of its body — so the hair sprouts up on the top of its back and sticks out over its eyes. But the cutest one of all is the long haired guinea pig, who looks like a mop on paws. Shown is a baby so its hair isn't too long yet. Guinea pigs come in white, black, brown, rust, gold, grey, spotted, and calico. They are nice to cuddle, and not too excitable. But when they get used to you feeding them, they will squeal and honk in a very silly way when they hear your footsteps coming towards their pen.

The pen can be a small rabbit hutch, or a plastic milk crate. They do urinate a lot, so you'll have to keep several thicknesses of newspaper in the bottom of the cage. and change it every day.

Guinea pigs, of course, are not pigs. They are rodents native to South America. And since this is a kitchen book, you might as well know that in their native countries they are raised for food.

# PART 4 —
# The Oven Takeover

# Old Stoves

Old stoves did not wear out. They weren't expected to, anymore than a house was expected to. It's hard to believe that the new-fangled push button electrics will be handed on for generations, or ever valued as beautiful antiques. But old stoves are. And plenty of people still use them. On the island where we spend our summers, most people have never lived in a centrally-heated house. Their stoves are the source of their heat. Some are meant only to give heat, like the tiny one called Sam in the photograph and the bigger cylindrical one. Stoves give off more warmth than fireplaces, because the heat comes out all around them instead of just from the front.

Other stoves are used both for heat and for cooking. The gorgeous huge one that the boy in the photo is cooking on uses kerosene for fuel. In the winter, it's lit all the time to heat the kitchen. It's perfectly easy to cook on, as long as you know how to start it.

If you're ever faced with a potbellied or similar wood stove, this is how to get it going:

1. Open the upper door and look inside. There should be a grate, with a well underneath it for ashes.

2. Poke around on the grate with a stick to get old ashes and charcoal to fall down into the well. Anything too big to fall through the grate — cans, bottles, partly-burned wood — should be removed. The grate must be clear because you need a draft from underneath it to get the wood to burn well.

3. If you find partially-burned wood, that may mean the well is too full of old ashes and must be emptied. Look for a door near the bottom of the stove, open it, and clean out the well.

4. Now check to see if there is a damper to adjust the size of the flue (or stovepipe) opening. The mechanism is usually a disk inside the stovepipe that turns to open and close the pipe. Look for a small turnable handle somewhere on the pipe. If no one around is familiar with the stove, you might have to poke around a bit to see what makes the flue open and close. When you figure it out, open it.

5. Put crumpled-up newspaper on the grate, add some kindling wood (small pieces of dry wood) on top of the paper, and light the newspaper. Close the door. As soon as the kindling is burning well, you can add larger pieces of wood. When they are

burning well too, you might want to slow things down and keep the wood from burning too guickly by partially closing the flue with the damper.

6. When the stove is going, don't touch it! Wood stoves get very hot.

By the way, if the stove you come across has a flat stovelid on it like Sam and the cylindrical stove in the picture, you can toast bread on it, boil water, heat things, and by removing the lid roast hotdogs and marshmallows on sticks.

# Cardboard Oven

It's hard to believe that you could really cook inside an oven made of cardboard boxes and light bulbs, but you can bake cookies, brownies and even cake — at 350°.

**You need:** **2 corrugated cartons (One has to hold a small oven rack. The other has to be a little larger because it will serve as the cover of the oven.)**
**heavy duty aluminum foil (the widest roll you can get)**
**masking tape**
**pocket knife**
**3 metal bulb sockets with twist switches**
**8 feet of double electric cord (the kind used for lamps)**
**snap-on plug**
**electrical tape**
**1-150 watt and 2-100 watt clear light bulbs (you can see the filament in them)**
**oven rack that fits the bottom of your carton**
**oven thermometer**

Line the inside of the bottom box tightly with foil (the shiny side showing so it will reflect heat). Make sure enough foil is left to be folded over the top edges and taped down with masking tape *on the outside of the box only*. Repeat using several layers of aluminum foil (you should probably wait until you are finished layering the foil before you tape them in place with the masking tape).

Cut your top box down to make a rather deep cover out of it. Line it the same way, folding the foil over the edges so you can tape it on the outside.

Cut three holes, evenly spaced, in the top of the box. They will hold the sockets, so make them small enough to hold the sockets firmly. Wire the sockets in parallel. This means the same wire is in contact with one terminal of each socket, and the other wire in

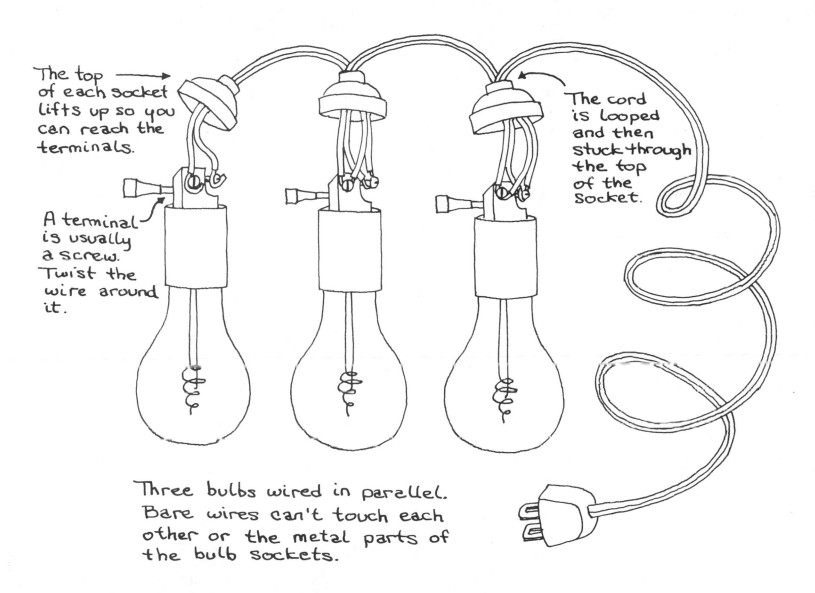

The top of each socket lifts up so you can reach the terminals.

A terminal is usually a screw. Twist the wire around it.

The cord is looped and then stuck through the top of the socket.

Three bulbs wired in parallel. Bare wires can't touch each other or the metal parts of the bulb sockets.

contact with the other three terminals. Use a pocket knife or paring knife to separate the two wires in the electrical cord, and to peel the insulation off the small areas of wire that must be in contact with the terminals. If you are left with exposed wires that might touch one another or the metal of the socket, you will have to wrap each carefully with electrical tape. Follow the illustration to get it right.

Replace socket caps, screw in the bulbs, put the rack and thermometer in the bottom, snap the plug on the end of the cord, plug it in, and you are ready to bake.

When all three bulbs are on, the temperature will reach 350° fahrenheit. The 100 watt and the 150 watt bulbs give you 250°. Two 100 watt bulbs give you 200°, etc. Switch on only the bulbs you will need to give you the temperature you want.

# The Easiest Cookie

The easiest cookie to make is Scottish shortbread. I've always thought shortbread was invented by a child since the recommended way to mix the dough is with your hands.

**You need:** 1 cup (2 bars) butter left out until soft
½ cup sugar (confectioner's is best but you can use granulated or light brown)
2 cups flour (don't bother to sift)

fork, knife, rolling pin,
cookie cutter (optional)
cookie sheet

Light the oven and set the temperature at 350°. Use your hands to mix the butter with the sugar in a bowl. Then add the flour and mix that in with your hands too. When it's all mixed evenly so you can't see any bits of butter or flour, it's finished.

What kind of cookies do you want? You can roll this dough into little balls or long rolls between your palms and decorate them with a couple of pricks of a fork. Or you can pat the dough flat on a cookie sheet, cut it into diamond shapes about half way through the dough and cook it that way, breaking or cutting it the rest of the way when the cookies are done. Or you can roll out the dough on a floured table and cut it into any shape you like with a knife or cookie cutter. We sometimes pat the dough into a pie pan and cut it into pie-shaped wedges as soon as it comes out of the oven.

Cook your cookies on an ungreased cookie sheet for about twenty-five minutes.

If you're curious about the word "shortbread" we'll share what we found out about it. Short is short for shortening. (Remember "Mammy's little baby loves shortnin' bread"?) Shortening is any grease like butter, margarine or lard that makes

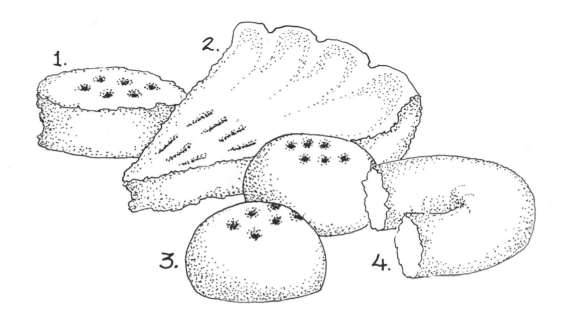

From left to right, these cookies are shaped by:
1. a cookie cutter    2. Pressing the dough into
a pie plate and crimping the edge with your
fingers    3. Rolling the dough into balls between
your palms    4. Rolling the dough into a cylinder,
cutting the lengths you want and bending them
into shape.  Holes are made by pricking with
a fork, and dents by pressing the fork tines
into the dough.

dough crumbly like these cookies or flakey like a good pie crust. But what does "short" mean? According to the dictionary, it means, among other things, short *of* something. Going a little further down the list of definitions, "short" describes a substance that crumbles because it is short of something that would make it strong. So shortbread is crumbly because it's short of something. But the only thing it could be short of that would make it crumbly is flour — add enough flour and it would get tough. So one is left with the conclusion that shortbread is short because it's not short of shortening. Enjoy it.

# Meringues

Although meringues are disguised behind a classy-sounding name they are nothing but egg white, sugar, and vanilla and are ridiculously easy to make.

**You need:** **6 egg whites**
**electric mixer or egg beater**
**1 cup sugar**
**1 teaspoon vanilla**
**waxed paper**
**cookie sheet**
**chocolate sauce or ice**
    **cream (optional)**

Light the oven and set the temperature now so it can heat up while you prepare the egg whites. A low-temperature, around 250°, makes white crunchy meringues. It also takes close to an hour to bake them. If you like your meringues a little golden and chewier in texture, try 350° and don't cook them so long. Experiment until you get them the way you want them.

While the oven is heating, beat the egg

whites with an electric mixer at high speed or an egg beater. When they begin to look frothy, add the sugar one spoonful at a time, and then the vanilla. Keep beating. The whites are ready when they stand up in peaks without drooping.

Put a piece of waxed paper on a cookie sheet and drop the mixture on it in small heaps with a spoon. You can make swirls or get points at the tops by fooling around with a knife or a finger. Bake them right away.

When they're finished, you can eat them plain or with chocolate sauce. Or, slice them in half and stuff them with ice cream for meringues glacées.

# Just Bake A Potato

If you can wait one hour for a snack after school, a baked potato is one of the best, cheapest, healthiest, and most filling things you can make.

**You need: baking potato**
               **salt and pepper**
               **butter, margarine, or sour**
                    **cream and chives**

Set the oven at 400° (450° if you're in a terrible hurry, or want a crisp skin to eat too). Wash the potato and put it in the oven. It's

done when you can pierce it easily with a sharp kitchen fork. You'll be able to smell that it's done too, because it will smell like baked potatoes.

Eat the potato with salt, pepper, butter, margarine, or sour cream and chives if you have them.

# Roasted Pumpkin Seeds

When you choose a Halloween pumpkin, test its skin with your fingernails. If it's thick and dents rather than breaks when you press your fingernail into the skin, you probably have found a pumpkin with fat ripe seeds inside. Most often a ripe pumpkin will be a big pumpkin — and you really wanted a big one anyway.

**You need: pumpkin**
               **baking pan**
               **salt**
               **butter**

When you scrape out the insides of your pumpkin next Halloween, save all the seeds in the membranes. Later, poke through this mush and pick out all the seeds. They will be slippery with bits of pumpkin shreds still

191

attached to them. Wash them in a flat pan, removing the shreds as best you can. Then drain and spread the seeds in a baking pan. Sprinkle salt all over them, and a few dabs of butter. Roast in a 300° oven until they are brown and crisp. Stir from time to time so they brown evenly.

Roasted pumpkin seeds are eaten shell and all.

# Sourdough

Sourdough bread has a faintly sour taste and a solid consistency that makes it different from other breads. Instead of buying yeast each time you bake, sourdough bread is made from a yeast colony that you keep alive yourself. This colony of live yeast plants is called a starter.

The whole process of making sourdough bread is going to sound complicated but once you've got the sourdough starter started, you can keep it going your whole lifetime. That is exactly what people used to do before they could run to a supermarket to buy yeast.

People even carried their starter all the way West with them in pioneer days. The more exciting way to start sourdough is to capture your own wild yeast. We've tried and tried and haven't caught a one.

If you think you'll have better luck than we did catching a wild yeast, mix a cup of flour with enough water to make it the consistency of a thick shake. Stir in a spoonful of sugar. Put it in an open jar on a windowsill outside in warm weather. If you live in a dirty city, several layers of cheesecloth over the jar will keep grit out but still let yeast in.

If yeasts come and colonize, the mixture will bubble up and smell "yeasty." After the mixture smells like yeast, double it just as you would sourdough starter, let it stand another day, and proceed to bake bread.

The easiest way is to begin with a package of commercial yeast. Make the starter three days before you plan to bake the bread.

**Sourdough Starter**

**You need: 1 package dry yeast
2 cups flour**

A cup of flour, a cup of water, sugar and yeast make two cups of starter.

Each time you bake, the starter is doubled by adding another cup of flour and water.

193

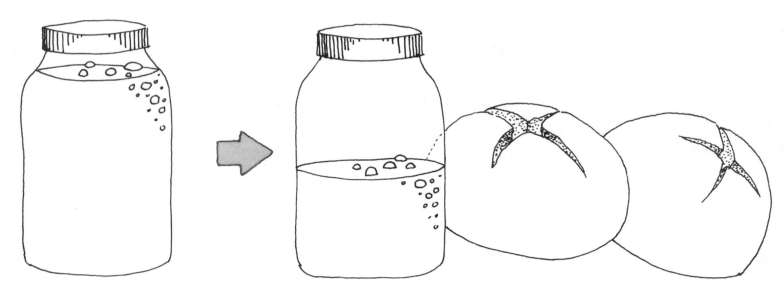

Two cups of starter go into the bread, so you will still have two cups to store and then to double for the next baking.

**1 cup warm water**
**cup, bowl, or jar with lid**
**1 teaspoon sugar (Sugar is**
**what yeasts feed on. Flour**
**has some natural sugars in**
**it but it won't hurt to add a**
**small amount of**
**granulated.)**

Mix the yeast, one cup of flour and water together in a cup, bowl, or jar. Cover the container. Keep it in a warm place like the top of a refrigerator for two days. The top of an older refrigerator is warm because that's where the motor is. (Newer models may exhaust warm air near the top or the warm air in a kitchen may rise and settle on the high surface of the refrigerator.)

The mixture will bubble up and smell more and more "yeasty." If it looks dead — flat and unbubbly — stir in a teaspoon of sugar, and be sure to keep it warm. It should revive. After two days of letting the yeast multiply, store the starter mixture in the refrigerator. This won't kill it, just keep it dormant until needed.

The day before you want to bake, take the starter from the refrigerator. Add the second cup of flour and a cup of water to double the quantity. Leave the mixture out so the yeast can multiply. You will use half this starter for your baking, and save half for next time.

## Sourdough Bread

**You need:  2 cups starter (put the other 2 cups in the refrigerator)**
**2 tablespoons melted butter**
**1 tablespoon sugar**
**1 teaspoon salt**
**2½ to 3 cups regular flour**
**butter to grease the bowl**

*Make the dough*. Mix all the ingredients except the melted butter together in a bowl. It is hard to know exactly how much flour you will need because flours differ. Start with two and a half cups and add more if the dough is too sticky to make into a ball.

*Knead it*. When the dough seems manageable, sprinkle a small amount of flour on a table or counter and knead the dough. Kneading is not as hard as some people say it is. If it isn't kneaded quite right, it won't make much difference anyway because sourdough

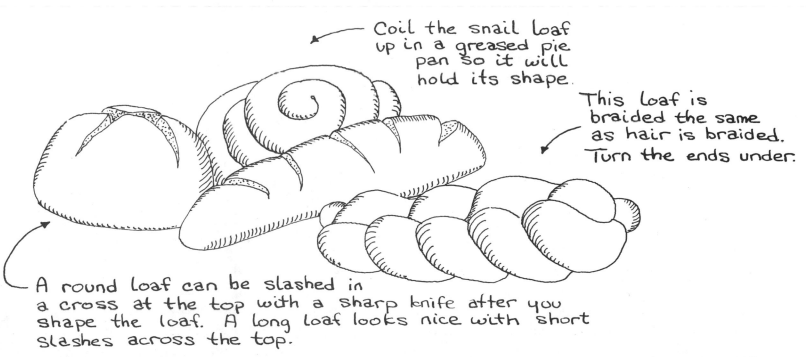

Coil the snail loaf up in a greased pie pan so it will hold its shape.

This loaf is braided the same as hair is braided. Turn the ends under.

A round loaf can be slashed in a cross at the top with a sharp knife after you shape the loaf. A long loaf looks nice with short slashes across the top.

bread is chewy at best. The dough is kneaded when it is smooth, elastic, a little glossy and you can see broken bubbles in it from the air trapped in the dough.

*Let it rise.* First grease a big bowl with some butter. You can do this with your fingers if you like. Put the dough in the bowl, turn it upside down so both sides have a little butter on them. Cover the bowl with a damp kitchen towel, and find a warm place for it like the top of the refrigerator. If your home is warm, you can leave it out at room temperature. Leave the dough alone until it is twice as big as it was. This should take about an hour.

*Punch it down.* Sprinkle some more flour on the table. Give the dough a few good punches to make it small again. Then dump it out on the table and knead it for two or three minutes.

*Makes the loaves.* Cut the dough in half and shape the two halves into two loaves of any shape you like. If the dough is so elastic that it won't work into any shape, let it rest for five to ten minutes. When dough rests, the yeast is busy making air bubbles, and in a short time the air bubbles make it spongy enough to shape into loaves.

Slash the loaves across the top in diamonds, crosses, or any other pattern you'd like. Make these slits only about a half inch deep; these cuts keep the loaves from splitting as they rise during the baking and also make them look good.

Let the loaves rise again. Put the loaves on a cookie sheet, cover them with a damp towel and let them rise again until they are double in size. This takes less time than the first rising. While they rise, preheat the oven to 400°.

*Bake the bread.* Bake the bread at 400° for ten minutes to get a good crust, and then turn the oven down to 375° and bake until the loaves are golden brown. Check them in half an hour, but it will probably take longer.

This is just one sourdough recipe you can try. Once you have your starter you can make any of the other recipes you might come across in cookbooks.

# Fake Bread

Fake bread is much easier to make than real bread, and though you can't eat it, it's beautiful for a dollhouse or to feed a teddy bear or as decoration.

**You need:**  **4 cups flour**
**1 cup salt**
**2 cups water**
**bowl**

**cookie sheet**
**egg yolk (optional)**
**liquid white glue (optional)**
**cornmeal, caraway, poppy,**
**    or sesame seeds, or coarse**
**    kosher salt**

Set the oven at 200°. Put everything into the bowl and mix with your hands. Keep squishing it between your fingers and squeezing it with your hands. If it sticks to your hands a lot, add a little more flour. If it's too crumbly to roll into a ball, or the ball has cracks, add more water to the mixture. When you feel the texture is right for shaping the dough, it probably is.

Shape the bread any way you like — round, French, braided, or oval like rye bread. A sharp knife is good for slashing the top of a loaf to make it look more convincing. As you make the loaves, put them on a cookie sheet, ready to bake. They have to be put into the oven within twenty minutes after you make them. Otherwise the outside dries out and begins to crack.

Set the oven at 300° and put the loaves in to bake. Loaves can take as long as an hour to get really hard — bigger things take even longer. When the loaves are done, they look an even toasty brown. If you want the bread to look really real, brush egg yolk over the loaves when they begin to look done, and leave them in the oven until they are the rich color of baked bread.

After the bread is cool, you can decorate it the way real bread is decorated. Brush some white glue over the top of a loaf. Sprinkle on cornmeal, caraway, poppy, or sesame seeds, or coarse Kosher salt.

We have had some troubles with our breads and other dough figures. No matter what you do, some of the loaves seem to split open as they bake. Make more than you need and hope for the best or try a lower temperature and just be more patient about how long they take. Humid weather makes them mushy. Try spraying them with clear varnish after they are cooked. But if you patiently wait for dry weather again, they will be okay. Also, although people can't eat these breads, our dog does — every time.

# Dough Sculpture

The same dough you use for fake bread is very good for making sculptures. Flat shapes work best because the dough isn't strong enough before it's baked to support much weight without falling down.

**You need: fake bread dough**
**            plastic staw**

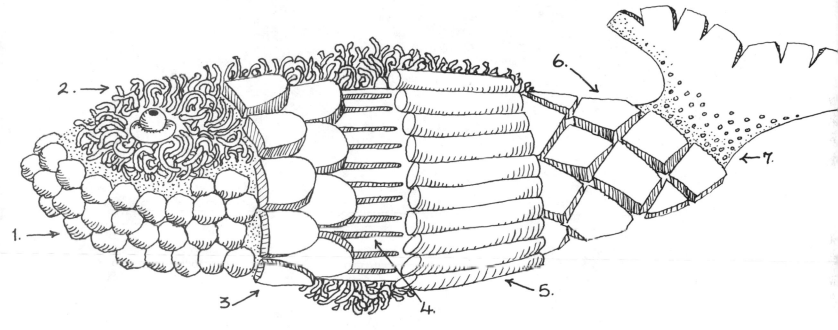

Beginning from his nose, this fish is decorated with:
1. Balls of dough   2. Garlic pressed dough   3. Flat scales pressed to shape from balls   4. Fork dents.
5. Dough rolls cut to the right length.   6. Knife cuts (they spread open during baking)   7. Toothpick holes.

Wet the surface of your sculpture when adding on pieces so they stick on well.

**acrylic paint**
**clear varnish spray**
**string**

Set the oven at 200°. Make about double the recipe for fake bread if you want to bake something big. If you choose to make an animal, try either a big snake, a crocodile, or a fish because you can make terrific decorations on them. It may take several hours to bake hard all the way through.

You can also use this dough to make flat shapes like cookies. Decorate them using the same techniques suggested for dough sculptures. Then cut a small hole near an edge by using a plastic straw as a tiny cutter. When the decorations are baked (they won't take more than an hour), you can paint them. Acrylic paint looks nice and is waterproof. Varnish them if you prefer they look like dough. Tie a string through the hole when you are finished and hang them from a tree or anywhere else you'd like a spot of color or art.

# Baked Beads

People like to decorate themselves with paint, feathers, cloth, and beads. This is a way to make beads from bones, dough and vegetables.

**You need: potatoes, beets, carrots or other vegetables**
**orange peel**
**vegetable peeler**
**fake bread dough (see page 196)**
**chicken or turkey neck bones**
**shellac or paint**
**carpet thread**

Light oven and set temperature at 150°. Cut the vegetables into chunks. Cut the orange peel into squares. In each chunk or shape, gouge a hole with the end of a vegetable peeler. If you have some dough left over from

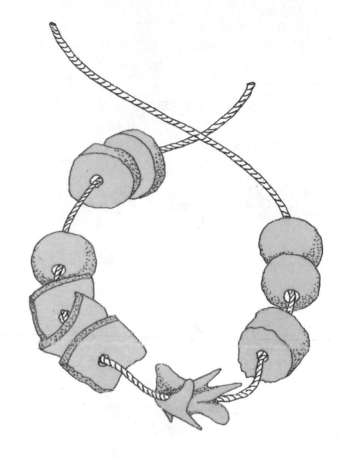

another project, use some of it for beads. Roll it into small balls. Use a plastic straw to punch a hole through them.

For bone beads, save a chicken or a turkey neck. Boil it for a half hour or more, until the meat comes off the bones easily and the bones come apart. Take the meat off and rinse the bones.

Spread your unbaked beads on a cookie

201

sheet, and bake them for about three hours. When they are done, the vegetables will be crinkled and leathery, the dough hard, and the bones brown.

Shellac will make them shiny and longer lasting. You can paint them too. String them on strong thread like carpet thread.

# Start Your Own Bread Business

This is the story of a boy who made $83.40 in five weeks by selling bread he made himself. Frankly, you can make more by babysitting and mowing lawns, but people don't admire you half so much. The boy's name is Lincoln. The bread's name is Portuguese sweet bread. It is a fancy, sweet yellow bread. It is so good that people keep asking for more than Lincoln can make.

**Portuguese Sweet Bread**
First, start with only two loaves to learn how.

**You need (recipe makes two loaves):**
- **2 packages dry yeast**
- **¼ cup lukewarm water**
- **1 cup sugar**
- **1 teaspoon salt**
- **6 cups regular flour**
- **big bowl**
- **3 eggs**
- **1 cup milk**
- **1 stick butter (take it out ahead of time so it gets soft)**
- **pan for baking**
- **kitchen towel**
- **extra egg yolk for glazing the crust**

*Start the yeast.* In a small bowl, mix the yeast into the lukewarm water with a pinch of the sugar. Let it stand in a warm place a few minutes, until the mixture bubbles up and doubles in volume.

*Mix up the dough.* Combine the rest of the sugar, the salt, and four cups of the flour in a big bowl. Make a well in the middle of the heap and drop in the eggs, the yeast mixture and the milk. Mix it all together with a spoon. Now add the butter and more flour and start mixing it with your hands because it will be getting too stiff to use a spoon. Keep adding flour until the dough can be shaped into a big soft ball — not too sticky to handle, and not too hard to shape.

*Knead the dough.* People act like kneading is some great mystery. It isn't. Sprinkle some flour on the table so the dough doesn't stick to it. Put the ball of dough on the floury surface. Put your hands on the ball of dough and lean forward so you're pushing the dough away from you. That flattens the ball. Now pick up the back edge, fold it towards you, and push away again. Fold it again. Push again. Every few times, turn the dough a little so it all gets kneaded evenly. When the dough looks smooth, shines a little, and has a good rubbery feel, you've kneaded it enough. It's not going to kill the bread to cheat a little on the kneading anyhow.

*Let the dough rise.* Wash and dry the bowl you've been using, and grease it with a little butter. Put the ball of dough in the bowl and then turn it upside down so both sides are greased. Cover the bowl with a damp kitchen towel. The dampness prevents the top of the dough from drying out and also stops it from sticking to the towel. Leave the dough alone in a warm place, like an unlit oven or the top of the refrigerator, for about an hour. By then it should have doubled in size. This is not a rule. We left the bread to rise overnight and that didn't hurt it. Other times we've put it in the refrigerator for a while because we wanted to do something else, and that didn't hurt it

either. It started to rise as soon as it warmed up.

The reason the dough in the photograph is running all over the place is that the photographer didn't like the light at 7 A.M., which is when the dough was just right for punching down, and made us wait until the light was better before he would take a picture. Meanwhile the yeast was growing like crazy, and you see what happened. It didn't seem to hurt the bread.

*Punch the dough down.* This part is the most fun. When the dough has risen, you get to punch it hard with your fist and watch it instantly deflate to a little ball of dough again. That's because you've slammed out all the air bubbles the yeast made over the last hour.

At this point the dough will be so rubbery you won't be able to shape it into loaves. You have to let it "rest" for ten minutes to let the yeast get some bubbles into it again. This will soften the dough.

*Shape the loaves.* Now you can shape the dough into loaves of any shape. Some suggestions include a "snail" loaf that was shaped in a pie plate, round loaf, and a three-strand-braid. Put the loaves on a cookie sheet or into pie pans for round loaves.

*Let the loaves rise.* Let the loaves rise again for about three quarters of an hour. Heat up the oven to 350° while the loaves are rising. The heat of the oven should make the top of the stove just about the right temperature for the rising loaves.

*Bake the bread.* Bake the loaves for about one hour or until they look dark gold and crusty. If you want them to look incredibly beautiful, brush the whole crust with an egg yolk stirred up with a little water at about the time the crust begins to brown (usually after three quarters of an hour of baking).

## Running A Bread Business

Making ten loaves isn't much different than making two. The kneading is harder work but everything else is about the same. You do need a very big bowl. The usual sets of mixing bowls definitely do not have one big enough. If you are serious about this, somebody will have to invest about ten dollars in a superbowl.

Another thing that's different is your schedule. If you start making the dough in the morning, you won't be finished selling the bread until late in the afternoon. There goes a whole summer vacation day. Lincoln made his dough in the evening, after everyone else was out of the kitchen. The dough was left to rise overnight on top of the refrigerator. Before breakfast, he punched it down and shaped it into loaves. After breakfast it was ready for baking. And by ten in the morning he was out on the street selling. It didn't take more than an hour to sell all the loaves, and then the rest of his day was free.

One other problem. Some ovens aren't big enough for all ten loaves. We got only eight into ours. Lincoln sold the first eight in the morning, then came back to bake the last two. These two, if he had worked things out cleverly, were ones that someone had ordered the day before and would come to pick up so we could all go swimming.

**You need (ingredients for ten smaller loaves):**

> **8 packages yeast**
> **1 two pound box of sugar**
> **1 cup lukewarm water**
> **5-pound bag of regular flour, plus another half a bag (or 2½ lbs)**
> **4 teaspoons salt**
> **1 quart milk**
> **1 dozen eggs**
> **1 pound of butter**

Lincoln made bread six days a week. After deducting the cost of the supplies, his weekly profit was $16.68. He worked for five weeks, so his total profit from his summer work was $83.40. He bought a calculator with it. We use the calculator for check book balancing, and income tax figuring, so maybe donating the electricity was worth it.

Now there is a certain psychology to selling very expensive bread. There is also a variety of delivery techniques depending on where you live.

*Delivery first.* Lincoln tried two ways and both worked. At home, where we are far from a town, he and a younger brother first took several loaves of bread to the nearest shopping center. They cut the bread in small pieces, had a little butter handy, and offered free samples on the spot. If a person liked the bread and lived reasonably close to our house, the boys took an order for a loaf or two of bread. When they got all these orders together, they worked out two different bicycle delivery routes. They delivered along one route Mondays and Thursdays, and along the other route on Tuesdays and Fridays. The bread was loaded into backpacks, but saddle bags would be fine too. Each time they delivered, they took (if they could get it) an order for another loaf or two of bread. The number of orders increased over the first few weeks as customers told friends and neighbors about the bread. It was a good steady business.

During summer vacation we live close to a town. Running the bread business there was much easier because Lincoln had only to appear on the main street at a busy time of day, and the bread would be sold out within the hour. There was also the advantage of having summer tourists continually pass through town — tourists like to buy things.

*Now psychology.* A basket looks quaint,

especially if it is lined with a nicely ironed kitchen towel. A hand-lettered sign attracts people, and there is something about ''Baked This Morning'' that has appeal. A personal touch is a good idea — ''Let me know if you enjoy the bread, Mrs. Smith,'' ''Oh you're having weekend guests, Mr. Johnson. I'd be happy to set a few loaves aside for you tomorrow.''

People may complain that the loaves are different sizes. They will be, because it is difficult to divide dough into ten pieces exactly the same size. So let your customers choose the loaf they like the best. Most likely each customer will choose the biggest loaf available. At last the smallest loaf will be left all by itself, and no one will be able to compare it to the others. However, if someone notices it is really quite small, lower the price and don't argue.

It is also important to have unused plastic or paper bags to put the bread into. Your local grocery store may cooperate with paper bags. If not, buy a roll of plastic bags.

If people complain about the price, explain that the bread is a special Portuguese holiday bread, that there is close to half a bar of butter and over one whole egg in each loaf, and that you would be happy to give them a special first time offer of a nickel off just so they can taste it once.

Of course, you could make a cheaper bread, but don't. Amateur bakers tend to turn out bread that is rather heavy because they have not kneaded it well or long enough, or have been casual about quantities, or have been impatient with rising times. So, if you make a plain old white bread, people might say, ''Good heavens, this weighs a ton.'' But if you make a very special bread, they will say, ''My, this has a wonderful firm texture.''

One last note for people who like a fuss made over them. If you live or vacation where there is a small town newspaper, you will probably get your picture in the paper. Twelve-year-old bakers are news.